BOSS CAT

ROY KEANE'S EPIC FIRST SEASON AS A PREMIERSHIP MANAGER

NICK BARNES

NONSUCH

First published 2008

Nonsuch Publishing
73 Lower Leeson Street
Dublin 2
Ireland
www.nonsuchireland.com

British Library Cataloguing in Publication Data.
A catalogue record for this book is available from the British Library.

ISBN 978 1 84588 918 0

Typesetting and origination by Nonsuch Publishing
Printed in Ireland, by Betaprint

For Joanne and William
and for Daisy
(who thinks football is stupid and gave
Roy Keane a note telling him so).

ACKNOWLEDGEMENTS

When I was a teenager I pored for hours over the sleeves of album covers dreaming one day of penning my own sleeve notes of thanks. I have not lived the dream until now. While it's not an album cover, it's the next best thing: a book.

I'd like to thank, first and foremost, Ronan Colgan at Nonsuch for having the faith in me in the first place and for prodding me in the right direction. He's been a rock. The book couldn't have happened without Louise Wanless, Martin Walker and Rob Mason at Sunderland AFC, and without the blessing of Andrew Robson and Doug Morris at the BBC.

Thanks are due to my colleagues at the BBC for putting up with me, not just over the past season, but over the years too: Simon Pryde, Martin Emmerson, Matt Newsum, Mark Tulip, Jeff Brown, Mick Lowes and Juliette Ferrington, and my long-suffering summariser, Black Cats legend Gary Bennett. Also Roger Tames and Georgie Frost, my colleagues at *Century* who've had to put up with me pre- and post-match, all season. Thanks also to Stuart Clarke of The Homes of Football for his years of unstinting support.

My thanks also to my colleagues in the press, but especially Graeme Anderson, a kindred spirit burning the midnight oil, along with Ian Laws, James Hunter and Nick Alexander.

Thanks to John Leech in Devizes who offered experience and encouragement and Julian Whitaker for his inspirational words in *The Horse and Farrier*. Finally, I would like to thank my mother, who doesn't understand football let alone like it, and my father who grew up watching the great Tottenham Hotspur teams of the 50s and 60s and took me to stand below the shelf in the 70s and 80s to watch Gilzean, Perryman, Chivers, Jennings, Hoddle *et al*. A footballing apprenticeship second only to following Sunderland.

If I've left anyone out I can only apologise, and my thanks go to you too.

INTRODUCTION

If you think you are beaten, you are.
If you think you dare not, you don't.
If you like to win, but think you can't,
it is almost certain you won't.

If you think you'll lose, you're lost.
For out in the world we find success begins
with a fellow's will
– it's all in the state of the mind.

If you think you are outclassed, you are.
You've got to think high to rise.
You've got to be sure of yourself before
you can ever win a prize.

Life battles don't always go to the stronger or faster man,
but sooner or later the man who wins
is the man who thinks he can!

These words, attributed to Walter D. Wintle, are posted on the dressing-room wall of the home team, Roy Keane's team, at the Stadium of Light. Not much is known about Walter D. Wintle. In fact it's not even known for certain if he wrote 'The Man Who Thinks He Can'. It seems it first appeared in a collected poems compilation in 1965. Curiously apt then, for this to be posted on a wall by a man we all think we know so much about, but about whom we really know and understand so little.

Kenwyne Jones, signed by Keane from Southampton in August 2007, has perhaps inadvertently summed up Keane as succinctly as anyone has done over the years. Having met him whilst a teenager on a trial at Old Trafford when Jones was seventeen and Keane thirty-one, Jones commented, 'I don't think the manager knows it but I have a picture of me and him back at home in Trinidad. Did he smile? No. He was being typical Roy Keane. Composed, picture, then move off.'

I was at St James' Park on the February afternoon in 2000 when Keane and Alan Shearer squared up to each other and Keane was (yet again) sent off. I, like many others I suspect, had a palpable dislike of the man. His shaved head and snarling menacing face oozed aggression. Of course, he was later to admit that when he ran out onto the football pitch he considered it 'going to war'. Even though, as a footballer, he was widely regarded as a genius, back in 2000 there was little to endear him to the fan. A 'genius' – the noun Keane himself uses liberally only when he talks about Brian Clough.

A year older, but having embarked on his managerial career at much the same age as Keane, is Gareth Southgate. As was the case with Shearer, Keane had his run-ins with Southgate on the pitch over the years, most notably when Southgate was with

Crystal Palace and Keane with Manchester United. In one bruising encounter Keane stamped on the prostrate Palace midfielder. Magnanimous or more experienced, Southgate now brushes the incident aside as being part and parcel of the game.

I first met Keane the day he was unveiled by Niall Quinn as Sunderland's twenty-fifth manager on Tuesday 29 August 2006 at the Stadium of Light. Quinn exudes charm and charisma, a presence unquestionably emphasised by his height and in direct contrast to the almost brooding aura that surrounds Keane. My first interview as a rookie radio reporter in 1988 had been with the legendary Blues guitarist B.B. King. Nineteen years later I was more nervous as I prepared to interview the Reds legend Keane.

The atmosphere in the room, packed with journalists, photographers and television crews, was electric when the pair strode through the back doors in their immaculate dark suits to take their places at the top table, in front of the anticipatory bank of cameras and reporters.

On the surface this was nothing new for either man, but the difference was that now both were embarking on a radically new adventure. One as Chairman – effectively a businessman – the other as Manager. Keane once famously described Quinn as a 'muppet' and neither had spoken since their infamous falling out at the World Cup in Japan and South Korea in 2002, until Quinn, aided by their mutual friend and agent Michael Kennedy, forged an unlikely partnership which was to lead eventually (and probably at times agonisingly) to this very press conference. In reality, their journey was only just beginning.

Keane dealt with all the inevitable questions about the World Cup with aplomb; Mick McCarthy, his temperament and the task ahead. He clearly knew he faced a challenging first season,

Sunderland sitting bottom of the Championship having won only one of their opening five matches. Their single win, against West Bromwich Albion, had only come the previous day, as Keane watched from the stands at the Stadium of Light. They had also already been unceremoniously dumped out of the League Cup by the Football League's bottom club, Bury, at Gigg Lane. It was after that defeat that Niall Quinn told me he was bringing a 'world-class manager' to Sunderland – a comment he later qualified with 'potentially', but nowhere have I read anything to dispute Quinn's initial claim.

Keane's achievements in his first season at the helm speak for themselves. Martin O'Neill, one of Quinn and the Drumaville Consortium's earlier targets for the job, said, 'I honestly believe he could be brilliant.' No coincidence, perhaps, that both O'Neill and Keane were apprenticed to Brian Clough. Of course Clough was a prolific striker for Sunderland, and had dearly hoped to manage the club one day. Ironic then, that fate was to dictate that Keane's first match in charge was against a club Clough did manage, Derby County.

That Tuesday I shook Keane by the hand and experienced for the first time that now familiar, intense focus as he listened to everything I asked and answered eloquently and intelligently.

Just over a week later we were to meet again, this time, though, *on* the football pitch. A 'behind closed doors' match had been arranged by one of the physiotherapists at Sunderland to raise money for an operation for a sick friend. The local journalists agreed to contribute by paying a fee to play in a team of reporters versus a team of Sunderland staff and coaches at the training ground, the Academy of Light. Little had we expected, that sunny September afternoon, for the Sunderland team to include Roy Keane.

I was a second-half substitute. It was one thing watching, reporting and commentating on football, but as a player I'd achieved no great heights. In fact the pinnacle of my footballing prowess was to appear for my primary school team as a defender in two matches, which we lost 12-0 and 8-0. Years later, as a striker, I did score for BBC Radio Devon in a 1-1 draw against the Met Office in Plymouth – a Met Office team that included the legendary BBC South West weatherman Craig Rich. Our team had, at one time, been 'managed' – a loose term which translated as 'cajoled' – by Ken Furphy, the former Watford, Sheffield United and Workington Reds manager, so as you can see I had a notable CV for the encounter at the Academy of Light. This is why I was a substitute.

I made my entry in the second half, coming in on the wing. I didn't get close to Keane in the ten minutes or so he was on though I prided myself on tackling Keane's assistant Tony Loughlan, nine years my junior, who was none too chuffed with my lack of deference. Keane sat himself down on a football to watch from the touchline, the touchline of the wing on which I was ploughing up and down. I hadn't ploughed as hard in years. The one thing I swore I wasn't going to do in front of the manager was slacken. Cardiac arrest would be fine, but slacken, that was a definite no-no. I was a relieved man to be replaced. Keane went back on, and it came as no surprise that his team came back from behind to win 2-1 with a penalty from the Sunderland kit-manager John Cook. As the game was coming to an end, I was gathering stray footballs behind the net of Kevin Ball. The legendary former Sunderland midfielder struck a lonely figure in goal as the remaining twenty-one players were encamped in the opposing penalty area. Then the final whistle was blown by the club's former assistant manager, Bobby Saxton, and in the distance I could see handshakes all round.

I began to stroll back towards the halfway line. Breaking away from the pack and waiting as the others strolled back to the dressing rooms, was Keane. He proffered his hand and said, 'Well played.' It may not have been true but it was clearly well meant.

ONE

Sunderland won the 06/07 'Championship' by two points from Birmingham City. Birmingham's manager, Steve Bruce, was the man assigned to be Keane's mentor when the latter moved to Manchester United from Nottingham Forest. Keane is selective about his friends but there's no doubt he has a great deal of time and respect for the Geordie, and texted him his support when Bruce was a beleaguered man earlier in the season.

Keane's phenomenal turnaround of his new club, from twenty-fourth to first, began relatively belatedly on 1 January with a 2-0 win at Leicester City. They lost only once more in the League from then on, at Layer Road, the graveyard of reputations, when Colchester United beat them 3-1 in April. The January signings of Jonny Evans and Danny Simpson on season loan from Manchester United, and the permanent signing of Carlos Edwards, the Trinidad and Tobago winger from Luton Town were key.

A big fortnight at the end of February and beginning of March was also vital. In those two weeks Sunderland drew at Birmingham City, who were then second; they beat league leaders Derby, at home, and won at West Bromwich Albion who were then top. It was during that match that Carlos Edwards suffered a shoulder injury that was to sideline him for a month. Jonny Evans, however, was proving to be a rock beside Nyron Nosworthy in the heart of the defence.

Nosworthy was one of the few survivors of Mick McCarthy's tenure as manager. The twenty-six year old from Brixton had been a journeyman defender at Gillingham for six years before McCarthy took him to the Wear, where he became a cult hero. He played thirty games in the ill-fated Premiership season when Sunderland amassed a record low of fifteen points. His characteristic surging runs from right-back, combined with his support act of finishing like a headless chicken whenever he found himself within eighteen yards of the goal, had won him plenty of friends but realistically, when Keane arrived and purged the squad, 'Nugsy' seemed an inevitable victim of the clear out. All the more so when Keane, as McCarthy had before him, played Nosworthy in his favourite role at right-back, sporadically, for the five months to January. When the transfer window opened though, it was centre-half Steve Caldwell that was sold to Burnley, in a move that underlined the new boss's resolve not to be mucked about by agents or what he saw as unreasonable wage demands. He also saw the disappointing left-back Lewin Nyatanga return to Derby County. In fairness to the eighteen year old, the only game he played in his favoured position as a centre-back was his last, at Leicester on New Year's Day, and Sunderland won. Following these transfers and an injury to the big Slovakian, Stan

Varga, there was a growing void at the back. A call to Old Trafford soon followed, and led to the loan signings of nineteen-year-old Ulsterman Jonny Evans and twenty-year-old Mancunian Danny Simpson. Both proved likeable and amiable and, especially in Evans's case, they seemed to have big futures ahead of them. On 13 January, Keane named Evans and Nosworthy as his centre-halves for the visit of Ipswich Town. Nosworthy remained ever present and Evans missed only one match to the end of the season. It came as little surprise when Sunderland fans voted heavily for Evans and Nosworthy in the 'Player of the Season' stakes.

It perhaps will come as no surprise to learn that Mick McCarthy had asked Nosworthy to play at centre-back, but he declined the invitation. When 'asked' by Keane, to decline would have been churlish – or just plain asinine.

One other mark of Keane's first season in charge, as well as getting the best from his players, was the number of late goals his team scored. In those final twenty matches of the season from 1 January – the period which really cemented Keane's management credentials – Sunderland scored in the last ten minutes on ten occasions. In seven of those matches, it was in the last five minutes, and four times in the last minute or added time, a notable characteristic of Premier League games.

The Premier League: The Holy Grail.

It was always Keane's intention to take Sunderland into the Premier League. As he reminded me on an almost weekly basis, it was the place to be. For him, it was the 'challenge [of] coming up against brilliant managers with great experience'. The former England manager Graham Taylor, writing in the *Daily Telegraph*, said:

> Getting promoted from the Championship – the old Second Division – was always the hardest thing to achieve in football. It still remains difficult, but staying in the Premiership for more than a couple of years after promotion is by far the hardest thing to achieve. It can be done, and Sam Allardyce at Bolton Wanderers is a terrific example to follow, but I suspect Keane will want Sunderland to be making their mark pretty well from the word go.

It was ironic that in the wake of Taylor's article, Sam Allardyce was to leave Bolton for St James' Park, thirteen miles up the road from the Stadium of Light. Taylor added, 'So next season are we going to see Keane's Sunderland challenging the top four? I have the feeling that Keane will expect nothing less of himself. He is special. Exactly what Brian Clough told me seventeen years ago.'

When the Premier League fixtures were published on 14 June, Sunderland's first match was at home to another team with top four pretensions, Tottenham Hotspur. After two consecutive fifth-place finishes in the Premiership under Martin Jol, Spurs had spent heavily (£40 million), a sizeable chunk of which was spent on striker Darren Bent from Charlton Athletic. Two seasons previously, Bent had scored twice in Charlton's opening-day fixture at Sunderland, and he had also been a target of Keane's. Sunderland had been no shirkers when it came to spending, their total falling not far short of Tottenham's, but it had proved to be a tough couple of months for Keane, Niall Quinn and Chief

Executive at the Stadium of Light, Peter Walker. At every club, the transfer rumours began on 29 April, the moment Derby County lost at Crystal Palace and Sunderland were promoted. At one stage, safc.com, Sunderland's official website, compiled a list of players linked with the club and it numbered over fifty. Keane remained tight-lipped. In appointing Mick Brown as Chief Scout, he had an excellent Lieutenant who at Old Trafford had unearthed such gems as Christiano Ronaldo, but as the summer wore on it became increasingly evident that any signings were going to come from closer to home. With due deference, there are few clubs less glamorous than Reading. Reading themselves had only reached the top flight in 2006, for the first time in their 135-year history. They did this with a points haul of 106 – one more than the record Sunderland set in 1999. Steve Coppell's team went on to take the Premiership by storm, finishing eighth in their first season and earning Steve Coppell the League Managers Association 'Manager of the Year' award.

The player to arrive as Keane's first signing of the summer was twenty-two-year-old right-back, Greg Halford. He had been the Royals' record signing, and the price of £3 million represented a profit of £500,000 for Coppell. This was perhaps a marker of what Sunderland would have to do to build a squad capable of emulating the Royals' success. Halford had actually only played three games in the Premiership for Coppell, largely kept out by the good form of Graeme Murty and then Ulises de la Cruz. This might have rung some warning bells, but Keane had rarely mis-judged so far in his transfer dealings. In fairness to Halford he had been very impressive against Sunderland for Colchester at the Stadium of Light the previous November, when he first caught Keane's eye with Nosworthy-esque surges down the wing.

Having seen Danny Simpson and Jonny Evans return to United, and with Sir Alex Ferguson making it clear he wasn't going to loan any of his young starlets again having been caught short as he closed in on the Premiership title, Keane was in the market for defenders. He signed six players on transfer deadline day in the August that he became manager and a handful more in January, so Sunderland fans expected another raft of signings in June. The silence was deafening but Keane played down fears, explaining that many players and targets were under contract with their clubs until 30 June, and that the French and Spanish domestic leagues had still to be completed – an intriguing hint of overseas targets. Once again, though, when signings arrived they were from these shores, and with a celtic bias. The Scottish international defender Russell Anderson arrived from Aberdeen with nine caps to his name, for a fee in the region of £2 million.

By now, however, it was apparent that Keane was being frustrated in his attempts to land some key targets. It also became inevitable that the names he was chasing would quickly become public knowledge. This, combined with the fact that everyone knew Sunderland had cash to splash, meant the clubs selling played hard ball. Not that Keane had a problem with that. Far from it, he told me, if he was to sell a player he'd want to get the best he could get too.

David Nugent at Preston North End was attracting several clubs. The Liverpudlian had scored thirty-three times in his ninety-four games for Preston, a ratio which his manager, Paul Simpson, said should have been greater. The twenty-two year old was said to be a firm favourite to sign for Everton but when nothing materialised, it was revealed that Sunderland had been given permission to talk to the player. He had pace and youth and was just what Keane needed at Sunderland. He'd also proved what he could do when he scored in front of Keane in Preston's 1-0 win at the Stadium of Light on 30 December. Nugent dilly-dallied though, and, annoyed by the lack of a response, Keane pulled out of any deal. Days later Nugent signed for Portsmouth. Indeed, close to deadline day Nugent appeared on the market again, with Derby County showing interest, as Harry Redknapp sought to raise transfer funds.

By then, however, Keane had made a move. To the chagrin of a section of Sunderland supporters, £5.5 million had been promised to Cardiff City for the former Newcastle United striker Michael Chopra. The twenty-three year old had hardly endeared himself to Sunderland fans in the last derby between the two teams, when he scored for Newcastle and set up a comeback which saw the Magpies win 4-1. Chopra then scored twice for Cardiff City at the Stadium of Light the following October and the gestures he made that night were clearly made by a man who didn't expect to come to the Wear. Firstly, he had just signed a lucrative deal at Ninian Park where he scored twenty-two goals in his first season, and secondly, as a Newcastle United fan he'd grown up loathing Sunderland. In Chopra, though, Keane saw 'a natural goalscorer'.

Keane's interest in Manchester United's Kieran Richardson was assumed as a matter of course, and there appeared little fuss over the midfielder's £5.5 million price tag. Ironically, Richardson was one of the players whom Keane had criticised in his outburst on MUTV which was never aired and which was the catalyst for his departure from Old Trafford. Since then, Richardson had enhanced his reputation with a good loan spell at West Bromwich Albion, though his efforts were in vain when the Baggies were relegated.

It was to West Bromwich Albion themselves that Keane went for another defender, another former United man. Centre-half Paul McShane had started out at Old Trafford, but failing to break into the first team, had moved to the West Midlands. Now at twenty-one he was forging a career with the Republic of Ireland. He had amassed five caps in the previous year and had become a target for a number of clubs. His fee was £2.5 million.

Keane was still trying to coax a goalkeeper to Sunderland. Darren Ward had excelled when he took over from Ben Alnwick in October, but his entire Premier League experience amounted to one game for Norwich City in 2004, in which they had lost 4-0 to Charlton. His understudy, Marton Fulop, was a Hungarian international who initially arrived on loan from Spurs. He then signed as part of Alnwick's deal at White Hart Lane but to all observers, including Keane, he was not the man to take over, and was duly despatched to Leicester City on loan.

Keane's target was Scotland international Craig Gordon. Ever since Steven Pressley had moved to Celtic, Gordon was one of the players who'd been publicly drawn into the row surrounding Pressley and the club's Lithuanian owners. He seemed destined to head south to the Premier League. The player clearly wanted to go, but Hearts wanted £10 million. The club was not inclined to let their prize asset and captain go cheaply, and for Gordon the experience matured him quickly, 'That's probably something that did affect me for quite a while'. He continued:

Last season there were some difficult times that I had to try and get through and being the captain of the club it was very difficult at that stage. We weren't playing well, we were losing games and there was managers coming in right, left and centre, so it was a very traumatic time for the players and I had to try and do my bit to try and help get the guys through it and get us playing well at the weekend … it was very difficult and I'd be lying if I said it didn't affect me and it did, because it was difficult, but I came through it and I think that's something that has made me stronger over time.

Sunderland were eventually forced to pay a British record of £9 million for a goalkeeper, just days before the start of the season. The parallels to the signing of Peter Shilton by Brian Clough in 1977 for the then-record of £250,000 were not lost. Shilton was signed from Stoke City with Nottingham Forest having just won promotion to Divison 1. Keane had actually decided he wanted to sign Gordon when watching a repeat on television of a Nottingham Forest game from 1978. 'Brian Clough spoke about how many points he reckoned Shilton was worth to him', he said, 'but Clough was ahead of everyone at that stage.'

Keane told the press when Gordon signed, 'as a player I probably underestimated the goalkeepers, but any team that has been successful has always had a good 'keeper'.

In between times, Dickson Etuhu, an experienced midfielder, had arrived a little unexpectedly from Norwich City and a young Irish winger-come-striker called Roy O'Donovan had arrived from Cork City. The twenty-two-year-old O'Donovan, who had also been a target of Fulham, encapsulated the Keane effect when he talked about Sunderland's pre-season tour of Ireland. The Irishman told *The Guardian*, 'I always followed Manchester United because Keane was there and I still do, but like a lot of people here, I also support Sunderland now. Quite a few fly over to watch Sunderland's games.'

A few weeks later he was playing for Sunderland rather than against them, as he so very nearly did for Cork City on 30 July before he was withdrawn from the squad after Sunderland had made their interest known.

Keane was *fêted* like a fifth Beatle as Sunderland spent a week in Ireland, playing matches against Bohemians, Cork City and Galway United. These came after games at home at Darlington, which they won 2-0, and at newly promoted Scunthorpe, which they lost 1-0. The Irish games saw them beat Bohemians 1-0, draw 1-1 with Cork City (arguably a chivalrous result in Keane's hometown), and win 4-0 against Galway United.

The last pre-season fixture pitted them against Italian giants Juventus at the Stadium of Light. The date for this game was the penultimate Saturday of the close season. Daryl Murphy gave Sunderland an eight minute lead but the Italians finished the stronger. Molinaro scored an eighty-eighth minute equaliser in a finale befitting Keane's team.

The opening game of the season was approaching fast, and on Saturday 11 August, the echoes and thoughts of Brian Clough resurfaced. 'He was an absolute genius', Keane said, 'He saw things before everyone else, buying players everyone thought were over the hill, but they won two European Cups with him. That gives me great hope.'

Keane's hopes and expectations for the first game with Tottenham Hotspur at 12.45 on the eleventh rested now with a crop of record signings, journeyman footballers, unproven young-sters and talented prospects. He hoped they would maintain the spirit and bond engendered the previous season in winning the 'Championship'. As a boy, Keane had supported Tottenham. Glenn Hoddle was his hero. As a player, he had turned them down to sign for Nottingham Forest. Now he was about to face them in his first match in charge. In the only place to be, the Premier League.

I want to create something at Sunderland. I want to leave my mark.

TWO

Out to the right wing to Whitehead ... and the whistle should go anytime, now ... here's ... on the right edge of the penalty area ... on the byline almost now ... Ross Wallace. Can he get a final ball in the box?

My voice kept rising as the seconds ticked away on my stopwatch in front of me; an old analogue Russian-made pilot's stopwatch on which you can watch the second hand moving round the white face, ever closer, tick ... tick ... tick ... I could hear it in my headphones, to the ninety-third minute, 'Into the penalty area ... Etuhu ... drops for Choprrraaaaaaa!' My voice, rising to a crescendo, 'YES!' I screamed, 'MICHAEL CHOPRA! It's 1-0 and he's won it for Sunderland!'

Standing in the tunnel afterwards, Keane, in his dark suit and his tie undone at the neck, no smile but an air of relaxing calm, told me, 'When I looked at him [Chopra] on the bench I knew he was keen to come on and then the goal was typical of him – fox in the box ...'

For Michael Chopra it was the dream start. Kept out of the starting line-up by Anthony Stokes who'd been impressive in the pre-season games, Chopra replaced the young Irishman in the seventy-second minute. When Chopra struck a side-footed shot from close range, three minutes and six seconds into added time, to beat a defender and England's number one, Paul Robinson, low inside his left post, Keane punched the air, throwing off the appearance of calm he exuded throughout the game. The only betrayal had been his jaw vigorously chewing gum throughout. Last season, though, Keane had told me that despite this apparent calm, he was like a duck, paddling furiously below the surface, trying to stay afloat. A few weeks later, before the home game with Blackburn Rovers, Keane admitted, 'I made the decision at the start of the season that I'd make a conscious effort not to be ranting and raving on the sidelines – it would probably have put me in an early grave.' He added:

> I see other managers doing it, but the road I want to go down is that, if I am going to lose my rag, I want to do it in the privacy of our dressing room. I've got to get points across, but on the sideline I see other managers ranting and raving and think that's not a road I want to go down. Not yet anyway.

Martin Jol was certainly not one of those who could be accused of ranting and raving, but he was omnipresent in his blue tracksuit at the edge of his technical area for much of the match. Afterwards, his distinctive face like thunder, he was angry at the defeat and, at odds with most, described the match as 'boring', singling out his strikers for both sympathy and criticism, 'I didn't feel they worked hard enough in the first half', he said, 'but then they didn't get the delivery.'

Jol had started with Dimitar Berbatov and Robbie Keane and ended with Keane, Jermaine Defoe and Darren Bent; Berbatov not at all happy at being replaced by Defoe in the seventy-seventh minute. But it was Sunderland who came closest to breaking the deadlock in the ninetieth, when Dickson Etuhu forced Robinson into a breathtaking diving save, tipping away Etuhu's shot which had looked like a certain goal. Craig Gordon had had only two saves to make. A long-range effort from substitute Tom Huddlestone, and, earlier in the game, a low shot from twenty yards by Robbie Keane. Afterwards, the Irish striker's namesake told me, 'You thought it was going to be one of those games where one goal was going to be enough and fortunately for us it came our way.'

For Chopra it was 'fantastic'. 'Being a local lad I know what it is all about in the north-east, but I think they love me now', he said, referring to any Sunderland fans still harbouring doubts about the Geordie's loyalty.

Martin Jol paid belated praise to Sunderland in his programme notes for Tottenham's home game with Everton the following Tuesday night, 'Sunderland provided a sharp reminder of the need to show more hunger and ambition than any of our opponents.'

Keane will have been privately pleased with that assessment from Jol, a manager already under pressure after just one match. His Spurs team of expensive all-stars had been firm favourites to hit the ground running, but this honour was to fall to Sunderland, just as Keane had hoped, and which they had deservedly achieved. 'Overall I never had any doubts about the players in terms of the talent and the spirit amongst them', he remarked in our post-match interview, 'but of course we have to go out and do it … the club have had disappointments many times in the Premiership, but I've got great faith in the players. But of course', he continued, 'I keep saying, it's a very good start for us but our season wasn't going to make or break today. We've another tough match on Wednesday.'

THREE

Understandably Keane was very relaxed at his press conference to preview Wednesday night's match at Birmingham City. He sat next to me on the dais in the media theatre at the Academy of Light dressed in his white t-shirt training top and shorts, and admitted he was looking at Andy Cole, another former team-mate, who'd recently been released by Portsmouth. With his arms crossed and legs outstretched he was *laissez faire* about the prospect of the Egyptian striker Mido leaving Tottenham to sign for Middlesbrough.

Mido, a month later, revealed he had actually been very close to signing for Sunderland. He is the first to admit he's full of admiration for Keane, buying his autobiography and even going so far as to read it all! In the Middlesbrough match-day programme before the game with Sunderland he said, 'He's a great man and could go on to be a big manager', adding, 'I was close to becoming a Sunderland player and I even met Roy Keane to discuss a move there but this is football … It was a tough decision because Sunderland is a big club'. Mido said he was 'very impressed by Keane because he is a very professional guy. He was honest and open to me and I was honest and open to him.'

That Tuesday morning at the Academy, though, it wasn't talk about Andy Cole, Mido, nor even of Birmingham City that got the journalists' tongues wagging. It was actually Keane's view on WAGs that made not only the sports pages but the front pages, the centre pages and even the fashion pages of the following day's newspapers and magazines. WAGs was the acronym for 'wives and girlfriends' that was adopted by the press at the 2006 World Cup Finals in Germany and Keane most certainly had a view on them. 'Priorities have changed in footballers and they're being dictated to by their wives and girlfriends', he delivered damningly, 'There's no getting away from that. This idea of the women running the show concerns me and worries me but it shouldn't because the players we're talking about are soft.'

Keane was obviously venting his frustrations, having not been able to attract the calibre of player he had hoped, in the main, to Wearside. 'We had a player this summer who didn't even ring us back because his wife wanted to move to London', he continued. 'He didn't even have the courtesy to pick the phone up to us and shopping was mentioned', Keane said. 'It's not a football move, it's a lifestyle move and they're the type you don't want at your club anyway. It tells me the player is weak and his wife runs his life.'

With comic precision a few days later Mido quipped he'd signed for Middlesbrough, 'because I like the shopping here'.

Before the Spurs match, Keane had berated a reporter for using the word 'survival' in relation to his ambitions for the season, but now, realistically, Sunderland were coming face to face with a team for whom survival really was everything. Two years ago, Birmingham had been relegated from this league alongside Sunderland. Bruce felt he was wiser for the event and better equipped to tackle the Premier League second time around. He was under no illusions about how tough it was, and had added Liam Ridgewell from Aston Villa, Franck Quedrue from Fulham, former Middlebrough teammate Stuart Parnaby and Johan Djourou on loan from Arsenal, in what was really a complete overhaul of his defence. Bruce also brought in Olivier Kapo from Juventus, Daniel de Ridder from Celta Vigo and Gary O'Connor from Lokomotiv Moscow, the former Hibernian striker costing £2.6 million. Fabrice Muamba's loan spell from Arsenal was also made permanent. Bruce managed to make these changes, while spending about a third of the amount that Keane had.

At St Andrews, Keane rang the changes. It was only six months since the two teams had last met here, but only four of the Sunderland team who'd previously started were on the pitch this time. The lucky four were Nyron Nosworthy, Danny Collins, Carlos Edwards and Dean Whitehead, and on the bench was Stern John. Liam Miller was to play in both matches as a substitute. The four 'rested' players, Dwight Yorke, Anthony Stokes, Daryl Murphy and Kieran Richardson, were all watching the match from the former director's box in the old grandstand in front of me, as was former teammate Jonny Evans and the Republic of Ireland manager of the day, Steve Staunton. Alan Curbishley and his assistant Mervyn Day, an old friend from our Carlisle United days, also made up the numbers, West Ham being next at St Andrews.

As was probably to be expected of two sides newly promoted from the Championship, it was a scrappy match. Keane agreed. 'Scrappy, I think, would describe the whole game', he conceded to me. A Paul McShane own goal had given Birmingham the lead against the run of play. It wasn't until the seventy-fifth minute that Michael Chopra equalised with a spectacular half-volley from sixteen yards, his left-footed strike whipping just inside Colin Doyle's left-hand post. 'I was speaking to Lougho [Tony Loughlan] before the game', Chopra reflected afterwards, 'and he told me that one of the balls is going to go over my shoulder and I'm just going to hit it on the bounce.'

Chopra, with two goals in two games, was now brimming with confidence, 'I've got a lot of belief in my ability … and it was just waiting for that one person to give me the chance in the Premiership, and thankfully it's Sunderland and the gaffer.'

Chopra's equaliser, however, was not to keep them level for long. Six minutes later Gary O'Connor, coming off the bench for his debut, put Birmingham back in front. In the eighty-third minute Carlos Edwards sprinted down the right wing and his perfect cross found substitute John, who headed onto the cross-bar. Edwards immediately pulled up with a hamstring injury. All three substitutions had already been made, so Sunderland had no choice but to play out the final minutes with ten men. In the ninetieth minute, Colin Doyle saved well from Michael Chopra's deflected free kick, but then John, a former Birmingham player, followed the ball up to head Sunderland's second equaliser from close range. 'We seem to be having a lot of these conversations', Keane said to me in the gloom of the tunnel behind the press room afterwards, 'about the players showing great desire, and keeping going to the end.'

A draw was probably the deserved result. Keane added, 'the performance … wasn't great. I had made a few changes to freshen it up, but after the weekend maybe there were a few lads heavy legged out there.'

A major blow to Keane, however, was the loss of the mercurial Carlos Edwards whose fond memories of St Andrews (he'd scored a wonderful goal there from twenty-five yards in February) were chastened by a scan a few days after the match, which was to reveal a torn hamstring. Characteristically Keane blamed himself:

> I take responsibility for that because Carlos hasn't done much pre-season and he had a tough game on Saturday, and tonight, so it was touch-and-go who I was going to bring on. Obviously it was Roy [O'Donovan for his Sunderland debut] who came on and maybe with hindsight I should have probably taken Carlos off because I knew it would be hard on his legs.

It was all part of the learning curve for Keane, who'd sent O'Donovan on to take the place of right-back Halford, who was struggling to acclimatise to the Premier League. Nonetheless Keane named Halford in the starting line-up the following Saturday at Wigan Athletic, and recalled the four who had watched the game from the grandstand. On the back of the win over Spurs and the battling draw at Birmingham, nobody was quite prepared for the calamity that was to unfold at the JJB Stadium.

FOUR

Before the match even started at Wigan, Keane had lost not only Carlos Edwards, but the talismanic workhorse, captain Dean Whitehead. Keane had a lot of time for the twenty-five year old, who was signed by Mick McCarthy from Oxford United in 2004. In fact Whitehead epitomised everything Keane saw that was good in a footballer; he had timekeeping, effort and professionalism, an all-round 'good attitude', and he had at one point been ambitiously linked with Liverpool. He'd started against Spurs at right-back, not a position he particularly enjoyed, but he never complained about being employed there when necessary. He had reverted to his favoured central midfield position against Birmingham, but a knee injury suffered in training meant he was going to have to sit this one out. As it transpired he was sorely missed.

Sunderland's only real attempt on goal came in the first fifteen minutes (during which they looked the better team), with Michael Chopra's twelfth-minute free kick forcing a good save from Chris Kirkland. In the eighteenth minute, however, Emile Heskey, whose impressive early-season form led to an England recall weeks later, scored from close range and from there it was all downhill for Sunderland.

In the second half Wigan scored twice more from the penalty spot. Antoine Sibierski was pulled down by Danny Collins, and then Heskey six minutes later by substitute Russell Anderson. Unfortunately Anderson had just come on for his debut in place of Paul McShane who'd suffered a deep cut to his forehead. Bizarrely, given that Wigan were awarded two penalties, they could have actually had four more. Referee Mike Riley waved away the first-half appeals, which, according to the general consensus, were all reasonably legitimate claims.

Keane's reaction was always going to be interesting. I braced myself at the pitch end of the tunnel and waited for him to exit the dressing room, which he did after around ten minutes.

'Fair to say Sunderland were second best?' I asked.

'Yep', was Keane's one-word answer. I pressed on.

'Poor passing, poor quality?'

'Poor everything', Keane replied, 'I can't think of any plusses to take out of the game, I have to say. Nope. I can't think of any plusses.'

Keane can't be faulted post-match. He never shirks the issues and, where he's generous with compliments when the team has played well, he is just as damning when they have been poor:

I do believe you need your setbacks … we learnt a hell of a lot last year. I remember Cardiff at home, Preston away … you learn a lot about your players, their characters and I certainly learned a lot today … I'm determined to get things right here and it makes me even more determined.

A mantra Keane had preached when he first arrived at the Stadium of Light was repeated at Wigan, 'Sometimes players help you with that [making decisions]. They help to make your decisions a lot easier, so a couple have done that today.' Watching the game from the stand had been Andy Cole. 'I think Coley just came as a fan to watch today', Keane added, 'so I don't know if that's helped, or put things in our way.' Ironically, before the match Keane had revealed he enjoyed going to watch Wigan Rugby League at the JJB Stadium because of the fierce competitiveness and the spirit the players embodied. This example was, it seems, lost on his own players that August afternoon.

Keane gives the impression that there are two of him. There is the after-match, heart-on-his-sleeve Keane and the pre-match, more thoughtful and reflective Keane. He admits that when coming straight out after a game he has not had the time to compose or articulate his thoughts, and what he says in the heat of the moment, with the adrenalin still pumping, can be very different to his thoughts once he's had a few days to analyse the game. Yet he is always quick to point out he doesn't like to analyse too much.

Without question, Keane's preparation for every match is thorough. Each player is provided with a DVD of their performance by Mark Boddy at the club and they work with a backroom team of fitness coaches and dieticians. This is coupled with the wealth of experience made available by Keane, Neil Bailey and Tony Loughlan on the coaching front. Sunderland are nothing if not professionally and thoroughly prepared. They would certainly have to be for their next match against the Champions League finalists Liverpool in Stadium of Light at the end of the week.

The paradox with Keane is that he strives for, almost demands, perfection, while at the same time, he is always learning from the mistakes he readily admits he makes. What he does do is try to marginalise the errors. He tries to reduce the risks, narrow the margins and negates the areas where things can go wrong. To that end it's clear he's digging deep into his memories of Brian Clough and drawing on the immeasurable benefits of his twelve years at Old Trafford. For example, he wants his players provided with everything to ensure a comfortable night's sleep before a match (within reason). Home and away, the team stays in a hotel ahead of the game, and if that be a softer pillow or a harder mattress, then the player will be provided for. The players then have less excuse for failing to perform and, for Keane, it narrows down the areas he needs to explore to ensure mistakes don't arise again.

Keane's approach to the Press underlines his professionalism. He is consistently indulgent and respectful, but won't be drawn into any arenas he doesn't want to speak about. Manchester United is unquestionably one of those zones. Also, any question of his professionalism will be met with a prickly silence or a one-word response. He confesses readily to his misspent early days at Nottingham Forest, but that is indicative of the catharsis that has moulded the Keane of today.

Strangely, despite the many cups and titles he won at Old Trafford, I think Keane feels let down by Manchester United.

He left at a time when the club was in transformation, as Sir Alex Ferguson was rebuilding his team and it was difficult for Keane because the players around him couldn't fulfil the high standards he had set and maintained. Keane talks of José Mourinho having raised the bar in his time as manager of Chelsea, and Keane had raised the bar at Old Trafford. Now he wants to raise the bar at Sunderland and, despite the calm exterior following the defeat at Wigan, his statement that he was 'determined to get things right' was never more heartfelt.

I have never encountered his like before. Keane combines an extraordinary drive and ambition, an all-consuming desire to succeed, with a remarkable benevolence. Rarely do we hear of his contributions to charity or his appearances on the doorstep of a disabled or ill supporter. It is not unknown for him to drive himself some distance to ring the doorbell of a deserving individual.

FIVE

Next up for Sunderland was a team that they would be lucky to get close to. After a bright start to the season, Liverpool arrived at the Stadium of Light on the back of a controversial 1-1 home draw with Chelsea (Chelsea's goal coming from a penalty that was subsequently shown to have been wrongly awarded by referee Rob Styles). Liverpool were now looking to score their 7000th league goal and they were to reach this landmark in the thirty-seventh minute, when Momo Sissoko scored his first goal for the club with a low eighteen-yard drive. Sunderland were finally despatched in the eighty-sixth minute, when Ukrainian Andriy Voronin, who arrived in the summer on a free transfer from Bayer Leverkusen, added the second.

Before the game, Keane had recalled his Nottingham Forest debut at Liverpool:

I had only just come over from Ireland and I was about eighteen or nineteen … I thought I was just going up to put the kit out, and that's what I was doing, when I was told I was playing … That was fantastic for me to make my debut – and of course I played my last game for United at Liverpool.

He also revealed that he'd decided to sign Andy Cole on a one-year deal, though it was to be sometime before the thirty-five year old would pull on a Sunderland shirt:

He has had a fair few clubs, but I have played with Andy and been in the same dressing room, and I know he likes to win. He is someone I have always got on alright with – it might be different now I am a manager, that might change … a player with Andy's history – you look at his goals record and his experience – he is someone we had to consider.

Experience was to be the key to Liverpool's victory, and it was only Craig Gordon, despite his relative youth, who kept the scoreline down. Gordon returned to the dressing room at the final whistle carrying Pepe Reina's goalkeeping jersey. Despite his impressive display, this was a brave thing to do in the week that Keane had admonished players swapping shirts with opponents. He had scathingly dismissed the practice, asking, 'how many medals have they got in their garage?'

A few weeks later, a tale emerged of how, after the game at Middlesbrough, Keane was in the middle of a post-match dressing down when the door opened to a Middlesbrough player clutching his shirt, who bellowed to one of the Sunderland players, 'here's your shirt'. Keane, so the story goes, immediately stopped talking and turned on his heels out of the dressing room. The players were left to consider the deathly silence.

A few days later a deathly silence was the last thing you would have heard in the away dressing room at Kenilworth Road.

SIX

Keane could have been expected to rest the majority of his first team squad for the Luton game, but this was not to be the case. In fact only three changes were made from the team that lost to Liverpool. In came Russell Anderson for Paul McShane, Grant Leadbitter for Dwight Yorke and, not unexpectedly, Darren Ward replaced Craig Gordon in goal.

Keane had signalled that the Carling Cup was a good route to success. It was a competition he wanted to do well in, and with Luton sixth in League One after only one defeat in their opening four games, Keane was treating them with respect. Three months earlier Sunderland had beaten them 5-0 at Kenilworth Road in their final 'Championship' match of the season, but the manager was taking no chances. No one could have predicted the humiliation that was in store.

Seven hundred and eighty-seven travelling Sunderland fans were left shell-shocked as Luton outclassed their illustrious visitors. Luton were one up after fifteen minutes when David Bell's free kick was driven through the wall. Thirty-eight year old Paul Furlong then scored two further goals and played the full ninety minutes, the veteran striker sensing a deserved hat-trick was on the cards. To compound the embarrassment, Greg Halford was dismissed for a deliberate handball in the second half. From Sunderland's perspective, the match was as shambolic as the stadium, which one reporter described as a 'dilapidated shanty'.

Keane took a while emerging from the dressing room, but when he did he was calm and magnanimous. On top of the humiliation, he revealed Dean Whitehead's injury was worse than first thought and a layoff of at least six months was feared. After the game he had also heard about the heart attack suffered by Clive Clarke, who was playing on loan for Leicester City in the competition at Nottingham Forest. The twenty-seven year old's collapse at half-time led to the tie being abandoned, and Keane revealed he'd given Clarke permission to play in the game, following Leicester's approach the day before. Less than a year earlier he'd given Stoke City permission to play Rory Delap against Sunderland at the Britannia Stadium, and ten minutes into the game Delap broke his leg in a challenge from Robbie Elliott. Taking everything into consideration, the night at Luton was one for Keane to forget. He left Luton reiterating his determination to succeed, echoing those comments made after the defeat at Wigan Athletic.

A day later he had some better news. Kenwyne Jones and Danny Higginbotham signed from Southampton and Stoke City respectively. The fee for Jones was £6 million, while Higginbotham transferred for £3 million. Ian Harte also agreed to a deal on a Bosman free transfer from Levante in Spain. The signings were timely. Next up it was Manchester United at Old Trafford.

SEVEN

On Wearside, one fixture counts above all others, and that is the derby with Newcastle United. But beyond Sunderland, as soon as the fixture list for the season was published, there was one match everyone was waiting for. The day after the transfer window closed, in a match inevitably moved for live satellite television coverage to an evening kick-off, Sunderland were away at Old Trafford.

Two days before the game, I was drawing into the Academy of Light at half past eight in the morning when a black Mercedes pulled up alongside. I looked across at the driver. It was Keane. I smiled and nodded hello. Unshaven, he barely managed a nod and a fleeting look of recognition before roaring off to the car park behind the Academy canteen and the seclusion of the trees. The security guard on duty at the main gate said somewhat rhetorically, 'Does he ever smile?' By the time Roy Keane came down to the media suite, however, he was clean shaven, relaxed and definitely smiling. With the inevitable interest in the match there was a larger presence than normal from television, radio and the newspapers, and after an intense forty minutes or so he arrived to sit down next to me and I asked him if he was fed up yet. 'No', he laughed, 'it's easier than working.'

Sunderland had lost their last three games and Keane again spoke of the need for patience, pointing out that Sir Alex Ferguson had taken twenty years to get the Manchester United board where he wants them, adding with a smile, 'of course having trophies helps'. As ever, he didn't expand much on Manchester United, but he was full of respect for Ferguson:

> He is clearly a winner. He was just motivated by winning, whether it be when we played the top teams or the bottom teams or a game of cards on the bus, he wanted to win. I love that in people anyway. I identify with people like that straight away and it's something I plug into.

For his part, Ferguson was to identify Keane's potential to be a successful manager. Talking in the lead-up to the match he said, 'Roy has the wherewithal to be a top-class manager. Some people can't make decisions. Roy can. I spoke to him several times about being a manager and when he started his coaching badges I felt he was doing things in the right way'. Ferguson was to go even further in his programme notes for the match with Sunderland:

> Roy Keane had the biggest influence on the team of any player I had at Old Trafford, and when Bryan Robson was coming to an end of

his playing career with us, my thoughts turned to the player we had monitored since he had made his debut for Nottingham Forest, at the age of seventeen, against Liverpool. We knew this was the kind of player who would do well for Manchester United but Brian Clough kept fobbing me off – and that's when I actually managed to get through to him on the phone! But there came a moment when we heard that Blackburn had been talking to Forest about Roy after Frank Clark had become their manager … I remember making a phone call to Frank from outside Macclesfield Hospital where I had been to visit a sick girl one Saturday morning before a match. I told Frank that Forest weren't being fair to us because we had been pressing our interest for some time, and that's how we managed to get him.

… Roy gave us a decade of superb service covering the club's most successful era and he contributed immeasurably to that with his drive and determination. Now he has taken those qualities into management and has done fantastically well at Sunderland. Promotion at your first attempt is no mean achievement and Roy seems to have seamlessly slipped into the manager's role. As a player, Roy always had a passionate and fiery image but now when you watch him he seems without emotion, a cool character – and I understand that because I'm that way myself. I don't smile, I look dour and unless we're five or six goals up I have no time for my surroundings. That's because I'm frozen into the game with a concentration that cuts out emotion. I see that intensity in Roy and it's a good quality.

Interestingly, Keane clearly delineates different qualities in Brian Clough and Sir Alex Ferguson: he refers to Clough as a 'genius' and Ferguson as a 'winner', illustrating an underlying warmth for Clough, and respect for Ferguson.

Potentially, Keane could have gone to Old Trafford and named six former Manchester United players in his starting eleven. As it transpired, only three started: Dwight Yorke, Danny Higginbotham and Paul McShane. A fourth, Liam Miller, was named as a substitute. Watching from the stand was a fifth – Andy Cole who sat with his son in the Director's Box. Another interested observer, for the second time in the season, was Jonny Evans, alongside Gary Neville and Ryan Giggs. Despite the absence of the suspended Ronaldo and the injured Wayne Rooney, the Manchester United eleven was strong and featured Owen Hargreaves, Anderson, Nani, Paul Scholes, Carlos Tevez, Rio Ferdinand, Nemanja Vidic, Patrice Evra, Wes Brown, Chris Eagles and Edwin Van der Sar. Amongst the substitutes was also Louis Saha, who hadn't featured since April having been injured in the Champions League. Before kick-off, the score from Anfield came through. Derby County, newly promoted with Sunderland, had lost 6-0 to Liverpool.

Keane was heading to Old Trafford having lost three games on the bounce, for the first time in fifteen years in football, and admitted, despite his relaxed approach, that it was tough. 'I have felt pretty bad this week but you get on with it, come into work and try to be positive, even if you have to fake it', he said, adding, 'Fake it to make it, as they say. I was doing that a lot.' This match would have the capacity to make him feel a lot worse but Keane was quick to point out that it 'is no place to go feeling sorry for yourself. Alex Ferguson has gone on to become a top manager by coping.'

Danny Higginbotham, who was to be given his debut in this game, spoke beforehand of the respect he had for Keane whilst a youngster at Old Trafford. Appearing also for the first time would be Kenwyne Jones. The 6ft 2in Trinidad and Tobago international was to be given a lone role upfront, supported by a five-man midfield. Michael Chopra was to start this game out wide on the right.

Keane's reception from the Manchester United fans was inevitable. It was always going to be good, and so it was. As ever, he was virtually the last out of the tunnel to make the long walk to the dug-outs, but the stadium, full as ever, was at a noisy crescendo, with applause and cheers for a man Manchester United fans had revered for twelve and a half years.

As much as Keane's reception was inevitable, so, unfortunately, was the defeat. However, fans' worst fears of being humiliated (which were heightened before kick-off with the news of Derby County's drubbing at Liverpool) were allayed. Sunderland lost to a relatively late goal from substitute Louis Saha, when Sunderland failed to deal with an in-swinging corner. That said, Manchester United were never in danger of conceding a goal and whilst Craig Gordon wasn't overly busy, Sunderland fans perhaps only harboured the hope they might watch a goalless draw. They had done so two years before, against the odds, when Kevin Ball was in charge. That same night, however, their relegation from the Premiership was confirmed, with what at the time was a record low haul of fifteen points.

Dwight Yorke, who started the game in midfield, was another returning face to the club he'd been an integral part of, having won with them, among many other things, the Champions League. 'I totally enjoyed [the game]', he told me afterwards in his laid-back, engaging manner, 'Like a kid again, going back to school for the first time. If someone said at thirty-six years of age I'd be back here playing again, then I'd have snapped it off.'

He didn't allude to exactly what he would have snapped off, but despite the defeat the pleasure of playing back at Manchester United was plain to see. Yorke went on to reflect on what the game would mean for Keane:

> It's a new stage in the management career where he's not had a lot of defeats in his time. The players haven't really achieved a lot of things in terms of not losing football matches so this is a new thing for all of us and we've got to learn extremely quick, very fast, and hopefully after this game we will understand what it will take to stay in the Premiership and start getting points.

Yorke continued to play a significant role throughout the season at Sunderland. Keane always pointed out how his personality was a big plus in the dressing room and tipped him to pursue a coaching career once he hung up his boots. He wouldn't even rule him out as being part of the coaching set-up at Sunderland in time.

Kenwyne Jones and Danny Higginbotham both looked bright on their debuts. Afterwards, Higginbotham admitted that, despite the prolonged attempts to prise him from Stoke, the decision to sign for Sunderland was a 'no-brainer'.

As might be expected, Keane played down the incredible welcome he had received from both sets of fans, but there's no doubt that it touched a chord:

> It's hard when you've lost a match, I have to say, but the fans' reception ... the Sunderland fans, you know that's always very nice but my priority and my focus is always on trying to win the football match. But I am grateful for the fans' reception.

An hour or two after the match as I walked back to my car behind the Stretford End, I was prevented from crossing to the car park outside the dressing rooms by a cordon of stewards. They were attempting to manage a large crowd waiting for Keane to emerge. He did so to a huge roar. Before reaching his black one-year-old Mercedes, he stopped to sign autographs and talk with a fan in a wheelchair. I slipped through the cordon and, as I drove off, Keane was finally reaching his car.

EIGHT

Ten days after the defeat at Old Trafford, Keane was to get a real sense of what Sunderland Football Club means to Wearsiders. Keane had insisted that the Academy of Light and the Stadium of Light had their walls posted with pictures of Sunderland's past, and the photographs of the 1973 FA Cup victory over Leeds United were a significant part of that tapestry. On 11 September, Sunderland woke to the news that their towering hero of 1973, Ian Porterfield, had died of cancer. Keane was only one year old when Sunderland beat Leeds but he instinctively knew how to capture the mood of the supporters, 'It's very sad news', he said, 'The word legend is overused in football but having scored the goal he did, Ian Porterfield is a Sunderland legend.'

Ironically, Sunderland's next game was against one of Ian Porterfield's former clubs, Reading. Before the kick-off on

15 September, the team of 1973 gathered pitchside, as the television commentary by Brian Moore of Porterfield's cup-winning goal was relayed around the Stadium of Light. The former players walked out to the theme of *Z Cars*, the old TV Cop series, as they used to do at Roker Park. The FA Cup was on show and 'keeper Jimmy Montgomery, whose double save from Trevor Cherry and Peter Lorimor in 1973 is legendary, could barely hold back the tears. A minute's applause was held before the kick-off, with current and former players ringing the centre circle amidst a highly charged atmosphere. During the ensuing match the stadium burst into a remarkable spontaneous crescendo of applause and chants of Porterfield's name. An extraordinary but extremely moving gesture.

As for the game itself, Sunderland won fairly comfortably, 2–1. Critically, it was a game Sunderland had to win, as Reading had had a relatively poor start to the season. Steve Coppell expressed his concern at the apparent onset of 'second season syndrome', having finished eighth in their first season in the top flight. Coppell said afterwards, 'Our position is a little oppressive. I have a list of reasons why I think teams don't improve in their second season but I'm not going to share them. It then becomes a self-fulfilling prophecy.'

One of the things that teams in Reading's position probably did have to do was to beat the teams around them in the table. Weeks from the end of the season, I calculated how many points the teams in the bottom eight clubs had taken off each other. At the top of this mini-league were Sunderland and Bolton, and at the bottom (with Derby) were Birmingham and Reading. At the end of the season both were relegated.

Keane will have studied Reading and Wigan closely, as he had every intention of Sunderland spending a second season in the

Premier League, but, as the months wore on, he was to find that they were facing a relegation battle. For the moment though, the win over Reading restored Sunderland's belief that they could compete with the middle-ranking teams. What he could have done without were the injuries to Carlos Edwards and Dean Whitehead. Before the Reading match, Keane told me:

> I'll try not to underestimate the loss of Carlos and the likes of Deano. If you'd asked me at the start of the season, two players you want to avoid having injuries, then let me tell you, those two players would be near the top and so are a massive loss to us, especially Carlos, especially now with Kenwyne coming onboard … there's no real player at the club who plays like Carlos.

A natural right-winger, Edwards was not to feature again until the Wear–Tyne derby on 10 November, but Jones, who scored against Reading, saw his star continue to rise. There was also some good news for Keane on the injury front. He revealed in his programme notes that the injury to Dean Whitehead was not actually as bad as first feared. Afterwards he was upbeat when he said to me:

> No one likes facing being out for six or seven months, I don't care who you are. I've been down that road before and sometimes you put on a brave face, but deep down you're thinking this is going to be a long road … that's why I believe it's not necessarily the physical side of it. It's the mental side of it and already I saw Deano there, and he's got a spring in his step and we're delighted with that.

Dean Whitehead made his playing comeback in a testimonial match at Falkirk on 15 November.

NINE

Next was a short trip to Teesside to face Middlesbrough, but three days before the game, the first high-profile managerial casualty of the season was heralded, as José Mourinho parted company with Chelsea. Keane was not the least surprised, but credited Mourinho with improving standards in the Premier League. He said:

> I have never come across him but I just look at what he brought to the Premier League and he raised the bar. He raised the bar for everybody, even for the likes of [Manchester] United, Arsenal … they had to liven up their act a bit and they came back stronger again, United and Arsenal, in the last year or two … The big thing for me is that he raised the bar for everybody, because maybe one or two people took their eye off the ball and he came along and thought 'I am the real deal' and that was good to see.

Inwardly, one suspects that Keane was sorry he wouldn't get the chance to pick the brains of his kindred spirit in the near future. In the meantime, though, he was about to come head to head with another rookie manager, Gareth Southgate, in a match that would be Keane's fiftieth at the helm.

To outsiders, Southgate and Keane couldn't be more diametrically opposed. Southgate had always been one of football's 'nice guys', while Keane had been the pantomime villain. Keane, though, was quick to play down Southgate's benign reputation when I spoke to him ahead of the game. 'You have to be tough and all the top managers have that. But it doesn't mean to say you cannot be nice. Look at me', he said with his trademark grin and carried on before I could offer a riposte, 'But I wouldn't be fooled by this idea that Gareth is completely 100 per cent a nice guy.' Keane then expounded on his desire to learn as a manager, giving a further insight into his obvious thirst for knowledge:

> I've met Gareth once or twice. I met him on a coaching course last summer and we had good conversations about, I suppose, the lack of experience we both have. Sometimes that's not always necessarily a bad thing, so maybe the conversations after the game will be different ... the conversation I had last week with Steve Coppell, or maybe after the match with the Liverpool manager, [they're] always different ... sometimes you are looking to pick the brains of the experienced managers, whether you're doing it quietly and you're hoping they're not realising it, or you're being really nosey saying, 'how would you deal with this?' But I have to say all the managers I've come across are always willing to help ... I was exactly the same last year in the Championship, coming up against managers – Dave

Jones and the Mick McCarthys – that have been managers for a long time, and I have to say they are quite helpful and always willing to pass on that bit of experience, because that's what you have to do. If you hold on to it yourself you stagnate ... when we played Liverpool I found Benitez very, very helpful and that's nice to see.

Sunderland salvaged a point at Middlesbrough, taking a second-minute lead through Grant Leadbitter but then conceding two, from two players who'd once worn the red and white stripes. The 'villains of the piece' were Julio Arca, a firm favourite on Wearside, who refused to celebrate his fifteenth-minute equaliser in front of the travelling supporters, and Stewart Downing, whose loan spell at Sunderland in 2004 led to his renaissance under Steve McClaren and his elevation to the England squad.

Sunderland's equaliser was a terrific shot in the eighty-ninth minute from Liam Miller. 'People used to compare me to Roy Keane,' he said, 'but only because we come from Cork and played for Man. United. We are different types of players, and he was world class.' Later in the season those words were proved far sighted, as Miller's timekeeping saw him fall foul of Keane. The manager had shown previously, with Anthony Stokes, Tobias Hysen and Marton Fulop, that bad timekeeping was a particular foible, when the trio missed the team bus to Barnsley.

Dickson Etuhu also collected his fifth yellow card of the season during the game, which meant a one match suspension. Keane remarked afterwards, 'I thought it was his fiftieth.' He went on to add, 'We probably scored too early and didn't know what to do ... we got sloppy and I have to say with about twenty, twenty-five minutes to go, it probably had 1–1 written all over it'. Keane told me he thought they probably deserved a point, 'I'd like to think so … I'm sure Gareth might think differently. Yeah, I think overall we deserved something out of the match.' Tellingly, with the way the season was to pan out, he added:

> If we'd lost today … I was sitting there thinking 'probably one step forward from last week and two or three back'. So it's like every point is going to be vital … when you're playing the likes of Middlesbrough and the teams that are around there with you, you have to get something out of the game. And when it's so late in the match, let me tell you, you take anything and that's the pleasing aspect. We can play a lot better than we did today.

TEN

Sunderland sat at fifteenth with eight points, three points above third-from-bottom Tottenham Hotspur, after seven matches. In the next few weeks Spurs, Bolton and Wigan were all to sack their managers, and the pressure was to grow on Gareth Southgate at Middlesbrough. It would be November before Keane's team earned another point but their performances belied their precarious position.

Before the home game with Blackburn Rovers, when he would come up against his former teammate Mark Hughes, I asked Keane if he'd spoken with him, or had any contact, since he left Manchester United. 'Nope. None whatsoever', was his succinct answer.

Keane was moved to vow he would not spend another summer like the one he had just passed:

In pre-season I was on the phone for hours every day throughout my holiday. I guarantee I won't be doing it next year. I
had to go through that to learn it. I'm pretty stubborn. I have to
go through something myself because that's the best way of
learning for me ... It was a complete waste of time because
clubs aren't prepared to do business when everyone is on
holidays.

It was a lesson he was to refer back to several times at the season's
close.

Grant Leadbitter's score in the eighty-ninth minute was too
late to rescue anything against Blackburn Rovers, who won 2-
1 at the Stadium of Light. Blackburn's second goal came after
Danny Higginbotham inadvertently played a poor back pass
to Craig Gordon, leading Keane to say, 'What happened today
we feared. Well ... it has happened and probably will continue
to happen until we get that bit more experience and obviously
there was a lot of naïve play.'

At the match I took the opportunity to sound out Graeme
Anderson, the *Sunderland Echo* Sunderland AFC reporter, for
his thoughts on Keane. 'I think Roy's unlike almost any other
manager, isn't he?' he said, 'In the sense that he's so incredibly
professional, but there is a line there you don't cross, but I just
think he's great for the club.' A couple of weeks later, we were
discussing the 'line you don't cross' with Damien Spellman of the
Press Association on a morning that he learnt Keane was having
a poached egg for his breakfast. Damien summed it up admirably,
'I wouldn't want to be the one to dip my toast in Roy's poached
egg.' Graeme Anderson continued:

He's been great since he arrived and I expect him to be great for years to come. I think people should cut him a bit of slack in the sense that he's only been in the job just over a year and no one gets to be the best straight away, even if you've been watching someone else working at the job for years and years and observing them.

Graeme has worked with many different characters at Sunderland, from Denis Smith, Peter Reid and Howard Wilkinson to Mick McCarthy and now Keane:

I think they should give him a bit of slack if results don't go as exactly as they'd hoped this season, but I think he could become – you know he's a legend at Manchester United – I think he could become a legend at Sunderland as well as a manager, and he is a pleasure to work with because he doesn't say a great deal sometimes, but every word he says is good copy for journalists. I know that talking to journalists who've covered the club for twenty or thirty years … particularly going back to the Lawrie McMenemy time, there were Sunderland-supporting journalists who said it pained them but they kept hoping Sunderland would lose because if they lost they'd get rid of the manager. There is an element of that, but personally I've never experienced it. I've enjoyed my job.

Both Graeme and I agreed with Damien Spellman who, whenever he was asked, 'What is Roy Keane like?' would reply with one word: 'brilliant'.

ELEVEN

Keane admitted that if he could pull on his boots for just one more game, it would be against Arsenal. Sunderland were to play for the first time at the Emirates Stadium at noon on Sunday 7 October.

Keane's rivalry with Arsenal, and Patrick Vieira in particular, is legendary. He told me:

It was brilliant, absolutely brilliant … Usually my preparation for a game on a Saturday, if we were playing Arsenal, would start on the previous Sunday. Your body just knew you were going to play Arsenal, just psychologically, your body would get ready for it. Those games were brilliant, absolutely fantastic, the best. United against Arsenal – if you could go back for one game then that would be the game.

Ironically, Arsenal at one time, like Sunderland now, had been regarded as having a strong Irish bond. Terry Neill was at the helm and the likes of Liam Brady and the current Sunderland chairman Niall Quinn were on their books. But as a player Keane battled with the continental Arsenal under Arsene Wenger. Keane continued in a philosophical vein:

> Stuff like that has gone. Those rivalries have gone. They still want to beat each other but there is not that real intensity that there was then. The game is changing. It is probably a lot colder. Football is not the game I knew maybe ten years ago and that goes for every club. It is changing and it is sad to see. But maybe it is up to the managers to try to do something about that, and keep their identities, keep it in the community and do everything you can … but yes, I would agree, football has probably lost its soul, certainly for the worse.

Keane, then, must have been heartened by his team's display against an Arsenal team that was unbeaten this season; a team that had won all their home games and conceded only two goals at the Emirates. It was also ten matches since Arsenal had conceded more than one goal and they were heading into this match looking for a tenth consecutive win.

After fourteen minutes, it looked a dead cert, as Robin Van Persie and Phillipe Senderos gave Arsenal a 2-0 lead with Sunderland being taken apart, seemingly in awe of the magnificent stadium around them. The Sunderland fans must have been sinking back into their high-backed padded seats, hoping the ground would open up and swallow them, but in the twenty-fifth minute Ross Wallace sparked an unlikely comeback, driving a low shot from eighteen yards past Manuel Almunia. The rally continued after the break. Three minutes after the restart, Kenwyne Jones rose to meet a Liam Miller cross and headed the equaliser from close range. The fans in the nearby corner were now delirious. Sunderland then rode their luck a little. Kolo Toure crashed a thirty-five-yard shot against a post and substitute Theo Walcott got himself in a tangle with an open goal just yards in front of him. With ten minutes remaining, however, Robin Van Persie finished exquisitely from a Walcott pass to put Arsenal 3-2 up. A minute later Sunderland's former Arsenal trainee Anthony Stokes almost levelled the score, but the young Irishman was denied, as Almunia brilliantly tipped his long-range effort over the bar. Sunderland were then further punished when Paul McShane was sent off for a lunge at Aleksandr Hleb, leading to his absence for the next three games, against West Ham, Fulham and Manchester City.

It had been a rousing match and, despite the defeat, the Sunderland fans had departed with their heads held high. Keane told me, in one of the myriad interview rooms off a corridor between the media 'theatre' and the players tunnel:

I try and look at the players' characters – their attitude – and that was there for everyone to see today. On another day we might have got a point but I think you need a hell of a lot of luck when you come to these grounds. They certainly don't need the encouragement of a two-goal start after ten or fifteen minutes. You need massive luck to get a positive result. We had a little bit of luck but maybe not enough to get the right result.

Arsene Wenger is renowned for not seeing incidents involving his players, and Keane, when asked about McShane's dismissal, effected a nice line in parody, 'I'd like to say I didn't see it properly, but I probably had the best view from everybody. I was about five yards away.'

With the league table now taking shape, Arsenal were on top and Manchester United two points behind. John Southall of BBC Radio 5 Live asked Keane if 'when [Arsenal] play as they did in the opening twenty minutes is there a better team in the Premiership?'

'Yeah. I would say maybe one more', Keane replied.

'Who's that?'

'Have a guess.'

'Manchester United?' John asked with a laugh.

'Yeah.'

'You think they're better and more rounded a team at the moment than Arsenal?' John offered.

'No. I wouldn't say better, but they've got qualities in terms of attack-minded players and it'll be an interesting game when they play each other. But my own personal opinion, and this is just my opinion, is that United still have the edge over them. But Arsenal are a young team and they're maturing very, very well, but if you step back and give players time on the ball then even you could play.'

Four weeks later Arsenal and Manchester United drew 2-2 at the Emirates; Arsene Wenger's team equalising in the final minute of added time. Manchester United went on to defeat Arsenal 4-0 at Old Trafford in the FA Cup and 2-1 in the Premier League, winning the title for the seventeenth time, four points ahead of Arsenal, who eventually finished third.

TWELVE

The Arsenal match had been Keane's fiftieth league game as a manager. It is a small landmark, which would have barely registered with the 'rookie boss', as he still sees himself.

There was a fortnight's international break before the next fixture, once again in London, this time at West Ham United. Before the weekend of the game, Keane admonished the written press at the pre-match conference at the Academy of Light. For some months the tabloids in particular had carried headlines accusing Keane of 'ranting', 'blasting', and so on, and he had finally had enough. It may not have been the fault of the journalists on the ground in the north-east, but of the editors and subeditors in London, but as they were the face of the papers, Keane naturally vented his frustrations. As he pointed out, he hadn't once ranted or blasted at the press since his appointment as the Sunderland manager. Far from it – the truth was quite the opposite. One or two of the journalists sub-jected to his berating quite rightly tried to fight their corner, but once Keane's mind is made up, it's made up. It was an argument he was going to win and he promised shorter press conferences and less co-operation in the future if things didn't change. In Keane's vocabulary 'No is a sentence.' Afterwards, everything went back to normal. Including the Sunderland away form.

Sunderland fell a goal behind to West Ham in the first half, but valiantly re-invented themselves after the break. Michael Chopra moved to partner Kenwyne Jones up front, and Jones terrorised the Hammers' back four. He soon scored a deserved equaliser but, in the face of a Sunderland onslaught, it all turned on a freak rico-chet off Craig Gordon. Former Newcastle United midfielder Nol Solano's introduction for West Ham in the seventy-third minute was the catalyst and five minutes after coming on, he broke away on the right wing, his shot striking the post. Unfortunately it bounced off onto Gordon's outstretched foot and rolled back over the goal-line. Sunderland were then caught on the break in injury time by another former Newcastle United player, Craig Bellamy, who completed a scoreline that flattered the home side.

Afterwards, as always, Keane took the time to pick the brains of his opposite number. Alan Curbishley was impressed by Keane. There were 'no moans', he said, from the Irishman, but blame laid squarely at the feet (literally in Gordon's sense) of his team's poor defending.

It was a defeat that meant Sunderland were clearly going to struggle. With eight points from ten matches, they sat a point above the bottom three and next up it was Fulham at home. Fulham were level with Sunderland on points, but their last away win had been over a year earlier, which was surely a good sign ...

THIRTEEN

In the week leading up to the Fulham game, Steve Staunton was sacked as the Republic of Ireland manager and, inevitably, Keane was asked for his opinion. Keane's views on the Football Association of Ireland are generally less than complimentary and, despite himself, he always has something to say, even as he admits, 'it's none of my business'. However, one could argue that as a former Ireland player and captain, and now a manager with a number of Ireland players in his squad, it is very much Keane's business. Despite the history between himself and Staunton at the World Cup in 2002, Keane was once again conciliatory:

I think we all appreciate what a hard job it is … for any manager, particularly for a young manager like Steve Staunton. It was always going to be a tough job. Unfortunately he lost the job like lots of other managers. I wouldn't say I have the word 'sympathy'. I think that's the wrong word to use, but I do appreciate what a tough job he had and, unfortunately, it didn't work out. We hope Ireland now pick the next manager, but I do believe that a lot of it comes down to the players, and a lot of the players, I feel, certainly let the manager down with their performances. Unfortunately we need to get some top players coming through.

Keane ended with a typically acerbic observation, 'having watched the [under] 21s a few weeks ago … I wouldn't get my hopes up too high'. This comment was sure to cement his current relationship with the FAI.

In Sunderland's last Premier League campaign they had failed to win a single home match until they played Fulham at the beginning of May. The game should have been played in the April but had been abandoned following heavy snow just twenty minutes into the match, with Fulham leading 1-0. The general consensus was they would have gone on to win the game had it continued and Sunderland would not only have finished the season with the lowest Premiership points total, but as the first team ever not to win a home game all season. The ignominy was avoided however, perhaps because when the game was played that May, Fulham were safe from the drop. Sunderland won 2-1. I could not help but use an old cliché, and ask Keane if it was a must-win game. Keane replied in familiar good humour:

I have to say, I feel like that since I got the job. Every game. I've never gone into a game relaxed, even when I got the job a year or so ago. Let's get away from the bottom [of the Championship] and let's try and get in the play-offs, try and get in the top two … this year we've had a decent start for the first week, but … I think every game's a 'must-win' game …

Considering Sunderland's failures away from the Stadium of Light, their ability to avoid relegation rested with their home form. Optimistically, at the start of the season, many felt Keane would have a relatively comfortable time of it and finish mid-table. It was now becoming painfully clear that wasn't to be the case. 'If we're going to have a decent season our home form is going to be vital', Keane echoed. He pointed out again that success or failure was very dependent upon picking up results against the teams around them in the table and, as the season wore on, there was a semantic twist in Keane's attitude to matches against the top teams. Rather than the publicly stated belief that Sunderland may get something against the 'top teams', the mantra became that what was required was that they 'put in a good performance'. Reality was perhaps kicking in. There's no question that inwardly Keane never believed that his team could easily beat the likes of Arsenal and Manchester United, but now, as he relaxed more in his public guise, he became more reflective about the size of the task he faced.

The players still certainly believed Sunderland would be alright. Only five points separated the bottom nine teams, though Derby were becoming marooned at the foot of the table. Bolton and Spurs were inevitably going to turn things around, or so it seemed. Spurs did, of course, but Bolton soon became mired in the UEFA Cup and a relegation battle. Spurs turned it round by controversially sacking Martin Jol and, eventually, appointing Juande Ramos. Bolton sacked Sammy Lee, less controversially, but, possibly even more controversially in the eyes of the Bolton fans, appointed Gary Megson as his successor. There's no substitute for experience, though, and Megson galvanised Bolton's home form. Like Sunderland, their dire away form meant they inevitably remained in the pack of clubs scrapping for safety.

Liam Miller emphasised the players' belief in their abilities. A very shy, nervous interviewee who talks barely above a whisper, he told me, 'We're frustrated. We're not coming away with wins behind us. We just need to keep going. There's no point in looking back … keep going and change that on Saturday. I really believe we will.'

The belief was slightly misjudged. Lawrie Sanchez's team took a lead just after the half hour from a Simon Davies free kick. One characteristic of Sunderland's frailties had been their failure to deal with set pieces. Next, in the second half, came the dismissal, for the second time in the season, of Greg Halford for a second yellow card. Halford's season had never really gained momentum and by January, Keane, whilst not publicly admitting as much, appeared to have lost faith in the defender. He was soon after made available for transfer, not even featuring in the squad following their defeat at Chelsea on 8 December.

It was left to Kenwyne Jones to rescue a point against Fulham. With five minutes remaining, he headed past Antti Niemi from close range for his third goal in three games. He wasn't to score again until 29 December but, if Keane had made a mistake in signing Halford, it was more than compensated by this signing. Jones was to become an immense figure for Keane – in every sense of the word. Afterwards Keane was sanguine, 'We'll look back at the end of the season and may see it as a point gained rather than two dropped.'

In the wider scheme of things, Keane had to be thankful he had Niall Quinn as Chairman and the backing of the Drumaville Consortium because while there were inevitably a few inner wobbles, they stood unequivocally behind Keane, always believing he was the man for the job. It would have been very easy in the climate of the Premier League to have buckled. By January, seven managers had been sacked and Steve Bruce had left Birmingham City because of differences with the board over his future and a proposed takeover which ultimately collapsed. He moved to another relegation threatened club, Wigan Athletic, who had sacked Chris Hutchings. Bruce could not be blamed for feeling it was a touch of poetic justice when Birmingham City were eventually relegated and Wigan avoided the drop. By January, the only other club in the bottom seven not to sack their manager was Middlesbrough, whose Chairman, Steve Gibson, was historically loyal and stuck admirably by Gareth Southgate.

The disappointment and frustration at the draw with Fulham was palpable. Expectations at Wearside had been high in the summer, even in the light of a history of false dawns, but the general belief that Keane was the man for the job was, in the main, unwavering. There were dissenters though. They remained in the minority but they were vocal. Keane and his team were jeered during the game. The jeers turned to cheers with Jones's goal, but critically the crowd had turned. They were to do so again in January following an abject defeat by Wigan in the FA Cup.

The Sunderland message boards became increasingly posted with opinions questioning Keane's judgement, decisions and tactics, but one of the manager's undoubted strengths is his ability to tap into the fans' psyche. He first had to do so after the Fulham draw, but he would have to do so again at Everton and following the FA Cup exit. Keane said with a smile:

> I was nearly booing myself ... it's unrealistic to think if you play badly you'll get applauded off. You'll always get a few fans that are disappointed. I was disappointed. The only way fans can show that is by booing. That's gone on for hundreds of years and will never change ... I played for a team that was very successful but let me tell you, if we didn't do well, we'd get booed.

In the end, Lawrie Sanchez failed to haul Fulham away from the relegation zone and in December he was sacked. The club stated that 'relegation was unthinkable'. Roy Hodgson was appointed his successor and was to engineer one of the most remarkable turnarounds of the league. He secured Fulham's Premier League status with only a few weeks left of the season, when they had been all but written off as certainties for the drop.

In the light of the draw against a team that many observers considered a 'soft touch' away from home, Keane needed to reassess:

> We'll need to look at all sorts of our training ... we didn't seem to have that energy and maybe we have been pushing the players too hard. You have to remember as well, in defence of the players, we're being stretched to the limits. Roy [O'Donovan] got injured in the warm-up and I don't know if the man upstairs is looking to help us out but we're down to literally sixteen players. Our full-back [Greg Halford] is now suspended for a couple of games. We still have Paul [McShane] suspended, so we're being tested ... and a lot of the players are playing with knocks ... for us to get a point out of the game

today, where you thought it's not really going to happen, it's credit to them for that.

Keane alluded several times in the season to 'the man upstairs' but, in an interview he gave to Tom Humphries of *The Irish Times*, he was quick to dispel the notion that he's a devout Catholic, merely suggesting he's a good Catholic boy. He said he observes the faith and takes his family to Church on a Sunday. Even so, it still probably makes Keane a rarity in football.

FOURTEEN

The next game was a week on Monday 5 November, Bonfire Night at Manchester City. The fireworks, however, were to be reserved for the dressing room afterwards. Sven-Göran Eriksson's team had won all six matches at home in their impressive City of Manchester Stadium – nobody, incidentally, seems quite sure whether to call it that or 'Eastlands', though the latter appears to be gaining favour.

Either way, a win over Sunderland would take Manchester City back up to third in the Premier League. How symptomatic then of football in the noughties that Eriksson was to face the sack in May following a tenth place finish and qualification for the UEFA Cup. Manchester City's owner, the former Prime Minister of Thailand, Thaksin Shinawatra, still deemed the season unsuccessful, further proof, perhaps, of foreign owners being out of touch with the roots of the English game. The Drumaville Consortium was prepared to buck this trend, even though at the end of the season Niall Quinn admitted to me they inevitably voiced a few concerns when Sunderland was teetering in the relegation zone. Credit is due to Quinn for reassuring the club's backers. In the end, they all stayed on board and confessed they wouldn't have missed the season for the world.

For any Sunderland players expecting a relaxing week following Keane's comments after the Fulham game, a shock was in store … before and after the game. Asked if he had reduced the workload, Keane told me, 'No. We have trained them even harder this week.' He spoke with an enigmatic smile and added:

> The players were probably surprised and shocked. Maybe they read my comments and thought they were in for an easy week. It's been really tough. It's been a tough week for them, I have to say. But we have got to look at it in terms of the bigger picture. When you have got nine days between games you certainly do not take it easy.

One thing became clear to me over the season – when you expect Keane to do one thing, he does the complete opposite. I laughed with Sunderland's head press officer, Louise Wanless, on a number of occasions when asking when Keane would hold his pre-match press conferences. We used to assume it would be on a Thursday morning, but if Louise made that assumption, Keane would invariably decide to hold it on the Friday. I know myself from my interviews with him that if I ever made an assumption about anything, he would beg to differ. The clear adage with Keane seemed to be to 'never assume'. I'm sure he's repeated that back to me a few times over the past two years.

Despite the harder training regime of the previous fortnight, Keane did admit that this week wasn't the time to change the overall routine. On the day we spoke, as an antidote to the more rigorous schedule, the players were being taken go-karting, as Keane sought to strike the balance between work and relaxation. It was turning into a difficult season, and a collective spirit on and off the pitch was important. Being the driven character he is, though, he added that there's no substitute for hard graft, 'There's a great satisfaction for anybody. You cannot beat going home knowing you have done a good day's work.'

A pattern was emerging when Sunderland were away from the Stadium of Light. They were playing as well as the home teams, but a lack of clinical finishing and an error-prone defence was costing them dearly. So it was to prove at Eastlands. On the day that Chris Hutchings was sacked as the manager of Wigan, Sunderland lost 1-0. The goal came from a sixty-seventh-minute Stephen Ireland strike, which was to become famous in its own right. In his celebrations, the twenty-one-year-old midfielder dropped his shorts to reveal some fetching Superman underwear.

Ireland was fast becoming no stranger to controversy. In September, just days before a game against the Czech Republic, Ireland had asked to speak to Steve Staunton and told him he'd have to go home because his maternal grandmother had died. Staunton agreed and a plane was chartered for the player's return. It quickly emerged, however, that Ireland's grandmother was not in fact dead. At this point Ireland announced it was his paternal grandmother who had, in fact, died. But, yet again, it was discovered that Ireland's paternal grandmother was alive, her relatives threatening to sue one newspaper that had, prematurely, reported her death. Steven Ireland's next version of the story was that it was a second wife of one of his grandfathers that had died. Ireland eventually came out with the truth, admitting he had invented a reason to leave the team in order to visit his girlfriend in Cork for personal reasons. He has not played for the Irish team since.

After the game, I asked Keane, who'd kept the players in the dressing room for forty-five minutes, if it was 'limp' to suggest they'd played well, since they'd gotten nothing from the game?

'No. I don't think we deserve anything tonight' he replied straightaway, going on to state:

> I have to say, I've been in football long enough to really earn the right to get something out of a game, and one or two balls could have broke for us, maybe in the second half, but we just didn't do enough. There was one real bit of quality in the game … that's what you get in the Premiership, and the lad Ireland took it very nicely.

Some months later, one newspaper was moved to write that the game had been the 'worst in the Premier League this season'.

Twelve matches played and nine points. Clearly this was relegation form. Next up, it was Newcastle United at the Stadium of Light, before an international break and a match at Goodison Park, which was to shape a lot of Keane's thinking away from home.

FIFTEEN

If there's one game you cannot lose as a Sunderland or Newcastle United fan it's the derby. This was to be the 138th; the first for Keane, and as it turned out, the first and last for Sam Allardyce. Allardyce had actually played a season for Sunderland back in 1980/81, when Sunderland were in the old Division One and Newcastle in Division Two. Allardyce had not won over Newcastle fans since his appointment in May, following the departure of Glenn Roeder, even though Newcastle United were sitting comfortably in tenth place and only five points off a European berth.

In the north-east of England, though, it's about style and substance. Keane had bought into this ethos and he seemed to know exactly what the derby meant. 'We need leaders. Warriors', he exclaimed. It was music to the ears of the Sunderland fans.

Sunderland-born midfielder Grant Leadbitter told me he was 'living the dream'.

Newcastle fans knew if Sam Allardyce adopted an attacking line-up at the Stadium of Light on the lunchtime of Saturday 10 November, they'd be favourites to win the game. He didn't. Even with Mark Viduka and Michael Owen starting the match in attack, Allardyce's tactics were cautious. Sunderland consequently battered their near neighbours for forty-five minutes. Some near misses and heroics from goalkeeper Steve Harper, born just down the road in Easington, kept it goalless at half-time. In the fifty-first minute the inevitable happened – Sunderland scored. Danny Higginbotham rose to head the opener at the favoured north end, right in front of the home supporters. (When given the choice of ends, Sunderland invariably elect to attack the North Stand in the second half. It is, perhaps, one reason for the number of strong finishes through the season.)

Newcastle United were barely in the game but they did equalise, somewhat fortuitously, in the sixty-fifth minute. James Milner's cross from the left swept in, off the foot of the post, in front of the 3,000 Magpie fans. A few eyebrows were raised again at Craig Gordon, who was still to convince Sunderland fans of his talent. Michael Chopra could have wrapped up a deserved win against his former and hometown club in the eighty-first minute but his shot came off the underside of the bar.

'A point gained or a point lost?' I asked. Keane responded:

Well I think the priority in any derby match is to make sure you don't lose the match, and we didn't do that, so we obviously learned from the other night. We were in a decent position in the game and we ended up losing. I'm delighted, but we're all in the game long

enough, we miss these chances then they come back to haunt you
– and that's what happened today.

Keane had no idea, that November afternoon, just how haunted
he would become just a fortnight later.

In between times, he took a squad to Falkirk for a testimonial
match and Dean Whitehead played for an hour to mark his return
to the fold. It was a strange evening, the game played against the
backdrop of the Grangemouth Oil Refinery, its glittering blanket
of lights twinkling across the wasteland behind the temporary
stands of Falkirk's incomplete stadium. The groundsman told me
before the game how a fox kept slipping in from the hinterland
and digging up the pitch.

Before I caught Kenwyne Jones and Russell Latapy languidly
reminiscing in the dugouts after the game, Keane spent a few
minutes taking stock on the season so far. It was always the case
away from the Stadium of Light that he'd be quizzed just that
bit more by journalists who were looking at Sunderland and
Keane in terms of the wider picture, and I don't think this made
him very comfortable. Tonight, though, he seemed quite relaxed
amongst the small group that had gathered pitchside:

> In an ideal world I think we could be [better off] – especially if you
> look at the [Manchester] City game. Even Blackburn at home and
> West Ham. I think we could definitely be three or four points better
> off, but we're not. But I'm very comfortable with the progress we're
> making.

Conscious of the number of managerial sackings already in the
Premier League – and it was only November – was Keane wor-

ried about his job prospects? 'Not yet!' he replied with a hearty laugh:

> ... that might change! No, no, we live in that environment where people are impatient and the way football is now, managers do seem to be getting sacked, and the strange thing is when they're sacked, it's like there's nothing new. There's no shock. It's just flashed across the television. That's it. And everybody moves on.

A week later, news flashed across our television screens of the sacking of the England manager Steve McClaren following a home defeat by Croatia and elimination from the European Championships. Keane added his thoughts to the mix, telling the press he backed José Mourinho and saying McClaren had been undermined by a number of players. He believed many of them had overstepped that fine line between ego and confidence, 'There're too many egos. Way too many. I could write down eight England players who have that trouble. We all could. In fact I could do twenty.'

SIXTEEN

Everton had started the season steadily. On 24 November, when Sunderland pitched up at Goodison Park, bolstered by the return of Whitehead and Edwards, things looked fairly rosy. Sunderland started with Whitehead at right-back, Kenwyne Jones and Michael Chopra in attack, and the experienced Dwight Yorke in midfield.

The Toffeemen, however, were rampant and took Sunderland apart. A hapless Paul McShane was targeted again and again, and the Sunderland defence's lack of pace was cruelly exposed. By the stroke of half-time Everton were 3-0 up. Yorke pulled a goal back in added time but it was a false dawn. Everton scored four more in the second half and could have scored a fair few more. The final score was 7-1.

A shell-shocked Sunderland trooped off from this mauling

with barely one of their fans left in the ground. Most had left with fifteen minutes remaining. By all accounts the dressing room was silent. An hour after the final whistle it was left to a Police Inspector to encourage Keane out, and then only because the Police escort for the team coach was about to go off duty. I'd been waiting without any great expectation of Keane making an early appearance in the tiny press room. When he did appear he was calm in outlook, but clearly hurt and chastened by an experience he had rarely, if ever, encountered in his playing career. When he spoke, he did so almost in a whisper:

When you look back on your career, you are going to have disappointments and setbacks, and no doubt this is one that's hurting me very much at the moment. But it will be hurting the players and the staff and the supporters just as much. It's not about my feelings today, it's about the club and how we react … you look back and say I've had three or four major setbacks and this certainly is one of them, 'cause we hope to do better.

Keane's intuition is to look forward. He rarely, if ever, dwells on the past, though clearly this performance would weigh heavily on his mind all weekend. Nevertheless he remained positive, 'We just hope the players react in a positive way. It's how we react, and I still have great faith in the players that they will bounce back in a positive way next weekend.'

To their credit, Everton, from manager David Moyes to Chairman Bill Kenwright, showed a great deal of respect to Sunderland, and refused to rub Sunderland's noses in it. This was something for which both Keane and Niall Quinn were very grateful. Whilst later in the season relations with Reading became strained, with Everton they became cemented. Subsequently, Keane shouldered the blame for the defeat, citing the wrong tactics. In persisting in pushing forward when 3-1 down, he insisted this gung-ho approach was a consequence of a lack of experience. It was to colour the way he planned for away matches in the future.

SEVENTEEN

Sunderland were now on only ten points from fourteen matches and, despite the seven goals conceded at Everton, had a goal difference of minus-fifteen. This might sound low, but it was thirteen better than Sunderland's next opponents, rock-bottom Derby. At the end of the season, they were to finish with a goal difference of minus-sixty-nine!

At this time, Derby had only six points, which included just one win, at home against Newcastle. They had not won away all season, nor even scored a goal away from home. In fact, coming into this match, they had played over ten hours of football without having scored a goal at all. Given this, it was perhaps unsurprising when, on the Monday before the game, they announced the sacking of manager Billy Davies. Paul Jewell was appointed as the new boss just in time for the game.

On the back of the Everton debacle, Keane inevitably rang the changes. Craig Gordon was 'rested', in the manager's words, not, as I suggested, dropped. Darren Ward replaced the Scotland international and Andy Cole was handed his first Sunderland league start. As many expected, Jewell's arrival galvanised Derby and they scrapped valiantly. In the seventy-seventh minute Carlos Edwards suffered a broken leg, which was to rule him out of the team until March. As it turned out, it was his replacement, Anthony Stokes, who was to be Derby's undoing. Two minutes into added time, in front of the North Stand, the young Dubliner struck. From a Liam Miller cross, Kenwyne Jones and a goal-line scramble, the nineteen-year-old substitute managed to hook the ball into the roof of the net to take the points.

For Keane, who admitted in the build up that following the Everton defeat, 'I didn't leave my house for about forty-eight hours, barely left my bed', this was a massive result:

> ... we've been speaking all week, forgetting about last weekend's disap-
> pointing result and performance, we knew that if we want to really do
> well in the Premiership, and at least maintain our status, then certainly
> we have to win the majority of our home games. Especially against
> teams around us. And we left it very, very late. But a fantastic result.

It was a quote which was beginning to ring with familiarity. Stokes's winner had been the sixth goal in fifteen matches that Sunderland scored in the final ten minutes of the game. In the previous season under Keane, they'd done the same ten times.

Ahead of Sunderland's next game against Chelsea, Keane admitted he was 'strapping himself in for a white knuckle ride' to preserve their top flight status. 'Definitely, like a roller coaster, like at Alton Towers, I tell you', he said.

Keane would perhaps beg to differ, but an inevitable defeat followed at Chelsea. Sunderland played well, but the afternoon was marred by the harsh and late dismissal of Liam Miller who reacted a little too petulantly to provocation from Claudio Pizarro.

In a bizarre prelude to the game Keane had walked into the press room at Stamford Bridge, which adjoins the dressing rooms, to watch the closing stages of the 12.45 kick-off between Aston Villa and Portsmouth. With one look he created a no-go zone around him, and he stood focused on the match.

This result meant that for the first time in the season, Sunderland had dropped into the bottom three. They had thirteen points from sixteen games, but crucially, despite their position, they were creeping towards a point a game. Historically, this average has been just enough to avoid the drop.

At this point Keane brought Ricky Sbragia back to Sunderland to help coach the first team. Sbragia had left Sunderland in 2002 after eight years as a coach to work with the Manchester United Reserves, including a side that involved Kieran Richardson. He left Old Trafford in 2005 to work alongside Sam Allardyce at Bolton Wanderers and when Allardyce left the club, Sbragia was seemingly left with no definitive role and so moved back to Wearside. It was an astute move by Keane who admitted that the fifty-one year old brought a cool head to the coaching team. When Keane and assistant Tony Loughlan were all for going 'gung-ho' in a match, Sbragia was the one who urged a bit of caution. His first step was to sink his teeth into stabilising the defence. Keane had taken a big step in bringing much-needed experience to the club.

If a white-knuckle ride had been promised, it was to be delivered against Aston Villa.

EIGHTEEN

By 15 December, Aston Villa had only lost once away from Villa Park. Under Martin O'Neill, who had been a Sunderland fan as a boy, they had moved into eighth in the league and were pushing for a UEFA Cup place. They were, however, arriving at the Stadium of Light having lost their previous two home games. The latest, against Portsmouth, was the game Keane had been studiously watching at Stamford Bridge.

In the tenth minute, Sunderland took the lead through Danny Higginbotham. They held on to this for another sixty minutes, but, with just over a quarter of an hour to go, the Scotland international Shaun Maloney struck a sweet free kick past Darren Ward.

It was deep into added time when Danny Collins rose at the far post for a left-wing corner and his powerful header beat Scott Carson in the Villa goal for the winner. I went berserk!

Seconds later came the realisation that the referee, Steve Bennett, had ruled the goal out. No one was quite sure why. Danny Collins pursued Bennett off the pitch seeking an explanation. The replays were pored over on the *Match of the Day* monitors in the tunnel. The goal had seemingly been disallowed for a foul on Carson, but the replays remained inconclusive. The assembled press and media became locked in the debate.

Exasperated, Keane pursued Bennett down the tunnel and vented his spleen. Witnesses described a foul-mouthed tirade and claims he had to be restrained by Tony Loughlan. When Keane returned to speak to me a while later he was clearly still smouldering. I meant to say he'd promised a 'white-knuckle ride' but instead it came out as 'knuckleduster'. Keane repeated my words, but sharply added 'to practice on myself', as he quickly realised the implications of publicly declaring that he wanted to use one on Steve Bennett.

At his post-match press conference, Keane told the assembled journalists, 'You say take him [Steve Bennett] out of the Premier League, but it would be unfair to the Vauxhall Conference and their players and supporters if he went down there.' Keane was clearly at risk of talking himself into trouble, as he accused Bennett of getting a 'big call wrong' and suggesting that he'd 'cheated' the supporters. He added:

> ... the referee was the only man on the planet who saw something.
> If he tells us why and gives an assessment then at least we understand
> why he's given a decision no one else on the planet has seen. You
> have to wait half an hour after the game to speak to him and who-

ever invented that rule is very clever. I'll just ask him. If he comes out with his reasons fair enough, but there's no logic to it. Nobody else was appealing.

I don't know if Keane ever did go to see Steve Bennett but I understand some nifty work by the club secretary, Margaret Byrne, and an understanding Mr Bennett meant Keane escaped the wrath of the Football Association. Within a week, however, Keane was yet again being driven to distraction by officials called Steve – this time the venue was the Madejski Stadium, and the officials were Steve Tanner and his assistant, Steve Rubery.

NINETEEN

At Reading, three days before Christmas, Sunderland were
fairly wretched. When the goal came, it began with a free kick
by Sunderland's January target, Stephen Hunt. The ball found
Ivar Ingimarsson at close range, who struck beyond the reach
of the recalled Craig Gordon. Ingimarsson then turned villain with eight minutes to go, tripping Kenwyne Jones in the
penalty area. It was a dubious decision, but nonetheless a penalty was awarded and Michael Chopra equalised with the
spot kick. Sunderland were heading for a precious point, their
first away from home since September. But, two minutes into
added time, Stephen Hunt turned a ball from the left goalwards.
Gordon appeared to claw it out before it fully crossed the line,
but assistant referee Steve Rubery judged differently and Steve
Tanner awarded the Reading winner. There was no time for a

Sunderland comeback. *Match of the Day* graphics later suggested it was not indeed a goal. From all the replays that I saw at the stadium, and the countless discussions afterwards, I was none the wiser.

I dreaded to think what was flashing through Keane's mind when the goal was awarded. I had visions of Steve Tanner being garrotted but when I spoke to Keane in the claustrophobic radio interview room at Reading he was remarkably composed. There was, however, something in his eyes that spoke of a fierce anger. He wasn't to be drawn into another controversy.

Sunderland were now back in the bottom three, but Keane was ambivalent about the prospect of the sack. Having seen his side denied three points by the decisions of the last two referees, he may have felt a degree of protection, but the real security came from the fact that Niall Quinn and the Drumaville Consortium were clearly behind their man. On the prospect, Keane said:

> It doesn't concern me one bit. If you get sacked, what is it? The end of the world? It's not. Top managers have been sacked before. Brian Clough was sacked after forty-odd days at Leeds and he wasn't a bad manager, was he? It doesn't bother me one bit. I wouldn't class it as pressure.

For all Keane's calmness in the face of the media at Reading, rumours abounded of a 'bust-up' that occurred later in Steve Coppell's office between Keane and Coppell's assistants Wally Downes and Kevin Dillon. Downes, a former Wimbledon player, is no stranger to controversy with a reputation for winding people up. This was highlighted the previous season in a very public touchline spat with the Sheffield United manager, Neil

Warnock. Keane was clearly on edge anyway, so it wouldn't have taken much to ignite the touchpaper. The result was a souring of relations between the two clubs. The water was not calmed by Sunderland's pursuit of Stephen Hunt, or Reading's attempts to lure Dean Whitehead away. In the past, two of Sunderland's best-known players, Ian Porterfield and Charlie Hurley, had been inextricably linked with both clubs, but it was clear now that they were unlikely to be the best of friends.

Christmas was looking gloomy. Scrooge had come to town and there was not even a ghost around the corner to remind Sunderland of happier times. The only thing haunting Keane was the prospect of their next match, on Boxing Day, when they would host Sir Alex Ferguson and Manchester United.

TWENTY

It was a humbling experience. Manchester United was three up by half-time, with goals from Wayne Rooney, Louis Saha and the brilliant Christiano Ronaldo. Manchester United took their foot off the gas in the second half but still added a fourth with a Saha penalty five minutes from time.

Keane gave a first start to seventeen-year-old striker Martyn Waghorn, a month shy of his eighteenth birthday. He acquitted himself well, but Sunderland as a whole were no match for their manager's former team.

Afterwards Keane likened his team to a boxer on the ropes, attempting to fight their way out of a corner. As well as a debut for Waghorn, the match marked the return of former Manchester United midfielder Kieran Richardson. He made an appearance as a substitute for yet another United alumnus Dwight Yorke. It was, however, Waghorn who created most interest. His inclusion took most by surprise, but not Rob Mason, the Sunderland programme editor. Only a few weeks before, he had featured Waghorn in the Aston Villa programme, following the youngsters hat-trick for the Academy team in the 6-1 defeat of Norwich City in the FA Youth Cup. This had been the first hat-trick by a Sunderland player at any level in the season. This Academy team went on to reach the Youth Cup semi-final, knocking out Liverpool on the way, but lost out to Manchester City. They then won the Academy League, but lost the play-off final, again to Manchester City.

Keane has always championed youth. Any former Manchester United player will tell you Keane took a keen interest in the youngsters at Old Trafford. Seventeen-year-old Conor Hourihane told me that, at Sunderland, Keane always stopped him outside the Refectory to ask after him and his well being. Hourihane strikes a particular resonance as he hails from Cork and Keane had personally persuaded him to join Sunderland after arriving on the doorstep of the family home. 'I've always had an interest in the young kids', Keane told the Club's magazine *Legion of Light*, 'and try to make sure I'm there to watch as many games of theirs as I can.' At the end of the season, when Sunderland's Academy team faced Gateshead in the final of the Durham Challenge Cup, they were leading 1-0 at half-time when Keane went in the dressing room. By all accounts what followed was the proverbial 'hairdryer' treatment. He came out some ten minutes later and said 'I just popped in to say hello'. Sunderland won 2-0 but in the words of one player, who shall remain nameless, they were too scared to actually lift the Cup above their heads for fear of upsetting the manager!

BOSS CAT

Martyn Waghorn played the full ninety minutes against Manchester United. Afterwards Keane told me:

> We don't necessarily look at players' ages; we look at what they're doing everyday on the training pitch. And he's been with the first team now and trained regularly recently and there was absolutely no doubt he would do well. And I thought he did very well ... in a very tough game for him. He looked assured. He looked confident, his touch. He didn't look nervous one little bit, and he seemed to enjoy it.

This was a warning, not just to the Academy players but to the senior players also. Everyone had to pull their weight. 'It does send a message to lots of players at the club,' he said, 'particularly the younger players and the people who work at the club, that if we feel a player's good enough then we're going to throw him in.'

Sunderland remained third from the bottom, three points behind fourteenth-placed Bolton Wanderers, the next visitors to the Stadium of Light. The match on 29 December not only marked Danny Higginbotham's twenty-ninth birthday, but a start for Kieran Richardson, his first since the Liverpool game at the end of August.

He was to start only a further four games before another hamstring injury after the home game with Portsmouth on 13 January, but he was greatly missed. In those four matches he scored three goals and proved to be an excellent foil for Kenwyne Jones, as well as a threat in his own right. Unfortunately, when he returned from the hamstring injury at the beginning of March, he seemed to find it hard to recover his form, and questions were raised about his future, but he had already played an important role.

Against Bolton, Richardson scored after only twelve minutes. He then turned provider for Jones in the thirty-second minute. Five minutes before the break, Sunderland succumbed to yet another set piece, a free kick from El Hadji Diouf. Diouf failed to score again in the Premier League until the penultimate game of the season, again versus Sunderland, which perhaps put thoughts of his transfer into Keane's mind.

The second half was played out nervously until Daryl Murphy finally put the game beyond doubt with Sunderland's third goal, in the ninety-first minute.

'It was a nice win', Keane told me, 'We had to win the game twice really.'

The result lifted Sunderland out of the bottom three, into seventeenth, and a point clear of Wigan.

'I have to say,' Keane offered, 'in other games we've played a lot better and not got results, so today it was nice for us to kind of grind the result out.' But what about Sunderland's propensity to drop deep to defend? I suggested that it was a habit they seemed unable to kick. 'Very deep,' Keane admitted, 'I'm sure our back four were behind our goalkeeper on a few occasions and you're always asking the back four to squeeze up, but it's easier said than done.'

TWENTY-ONE

The January transfer window was now open, but there were to be no new faces in time for the next match. On the evening of 2 January, a bitterly cold night, Sunderland travelled to Blackburn Rovers. Keane played a new formation at Ewood Park as he continued to search for that elusive away win. Dwight Yorke, returning to another of his former clubs, sat in front of the back four and Kenwyne Jones played on his own up front. It seemed to be working well as Sunderland dominated the first half. Five minutes into the second half, Sunderland won a penalty but captain Dean Whitehead, refusing Yorke's appeal to take the kick, struck a feeble shot which Brad Friedel saved comfortably. This was the game's turning point. Five minutes later Danny Higginbotham was harshly punished for a handball by referee Rob Styles, and Benni McCarthy illustrated how penalties should be taken.

Adding insult to injury, Dwight Yorke was sent off in the seventi-
eth minute after collecting two yellow cards in as many minutes.

Sunderland beat themselves and Keane wasn't about to disa-
gree. 'There were opportunities there for us to win the game',
he said in the tunnel, just outside Rob Styles's dressing room. I
listened to him while standing as close as possible to a fan heater
perched on top of a table. 'Certainly not to lose it', Keane continued as I shivered in front of him, 'But we shot ourselves in
the foot. We had a chance to get in front, don't take it and in a
few minutes we're a goal behind. As you said there, there was an
opportunity to get something out of the game.'

Sunderland were back in the bottom three now, three points
behind Wigan, who they would face next in the third round of
the FA Cup. This was clearly a season that was going to throw up
all manner of upsets for Keane.

Five changes were made for the cup game. Nyron Nosworthy
returned at right-back after a month's absence. Martyn Waghorn
started up front alongside Daryl Murphy, and Roy O'Donovan
started only his second game on the right-wing. The attendance
for the game was not huge, a disappointing 20,821. As O'Donovan
remarked afterwards, he 'played in front of one man and his dog
in the League of Ireland', and was happy just to be on the pitch.
Graham Kavanagh, between loan spells, also played his one and
only game of this season, and won the man of the match award
for his performance. In the circumstances, it was not an accolade
to be proud of. Sunderland were simply dreadful and lost 3-0.

Keane was simmering with anger, 'We've played Wigan twice
now and conceded six goals and not scored. Clearly that's not
good enough.' There had been criticism that Keane had not taken
the tie seriously, but he was adamant that was not the case:

I know there's a lot made of the FA Cup this week, but we certainly approached the game and we tried to win … I think we'd have been there to midnight and we wouldn't have scored tonight. I've said to many of these people [who say the Cup is not a priority] that if they got to an FA Cup final maybe that will change. I can't get my head round it … we prepared as well as we normally do. Last night, the usual. We picked the team, we didn't cut any corners and it was a flat atmosphere, but having said that sometimes it's up to the players to make it happen …

Wigan did not go on to lift the cup, and, for the first time in 100 years only one club from the top flight, Portsmouth, was to actually reach the last four of this competition. The remaining three, Barnsley, Cardiff and West Bromwich Albion, were all in the Championship. The Premier League top-four's grip on the cup was broken and this was welcomed by just about everybody.

As if the result wasn't bad enough, the weekend soon got worse for Keane. Clive Clarke, who'd collapsed at Nottingham Forest the night Sunderland were crashing out of the League Cup at Luton, was reported in an Irish newspaper claiming Keane was undermining the confidence of his players by refusing to speak to them. Clarke said, 'I spoke to him a couple of times at the club and he rang me when it happened, which was very nice of him, but we're not very pally.'

No surprise there, but what really set the cat amongst the pigeons was the claim Keane was 'going around booting chairs and throwing things'. These quotes were denied by Clarke. At best it seems they were taken out of context. At worst they were spoken in frustration and contained some germ of truth. Clearly, Keane was under the spotlight with Sunderland struggling in the Premier League and with a high profile in his homeland. Keane played down the reports and dismissed them as irrelevant but Clarke was nonetheless fined and a few months later left the club.

At the same time, a report appeared in the *Sunday Mirror* claiming Anthony Stokes was playing loud music at home and disturbing his elderly neighbour, who had been driven to appeal directly to Keane to sort it out. Needless to say, she wasn't troubled again.

TWENTY-TWO

On 9 January, to everyone's surprise bar perhaps Keane, Sam Allardyce was sacked by Newcastle United. The Portsmouth manager Harry Redknapp was favourite to succeed him and the run up to Sunderland's home game with Portsmouth on the Sunday 13 January was dominated by almost comical blanket coverage of this debate. The 'will he or won't he, has he or hasn't he, where is he now?' conjecture came to an abrupt end on the Sunday morning when the sixty year old rejected decisively Newcastle's overtures. He then took charge at the Stadium of Light for a match in which Keane promised we'd see the 'true Sunderland'.

Portsmouth, crucially, having won seven away games already – a record they shared only with Chelsea – were without four key players. The players, who were on Africa Cup of Nations duty, included the influential Sulley Muntari and striker Kanu. Nevertheless, they still had Benjani who had scored nine goals to date in the Premier League.

Keane took this opportunity to give a debut to his first signing of the transfer window. He had persuaded Sir Alex Ferguson to release centre-half Jonny Evans until the end of the season. The twenty year old had been a major loan signing for Keane the previous January and, a year to the day later, Evans returned. He had been at the centre of some lurid headlines and allegations after Manchester United's Christmas party, but at Sunderland he was all business. The previous season he had developed an outstanding partnership with Nosworthy in the centre of defence, and this partnership was to prove equally durable in the Premier League.

A brace from Kieran Richardson gave Sunderland a 2-0 win. Kenwyne Jones was outstanding in front of his former Southampton manager, and it was his perseverance, chasing a ball given up for dead by Sol Campbell, that led to the opening goal. Richardson was denied a hat-trick on the hour mark only by the crossbar.

The best performance of the season? I asked Keane.

Possibly so, possibly so. Against a good Portsmouth team who are, away from home, very good. No doubt they're missing three or four players, of course, and we've got to be respectful of that, but having said that, Wigan were missing a few last week and we didn't take advantage ... you still have to make the most of it and we scored two cracking goals.

The win failed to lift Sunderland out of the bottom three, but they were now level on twenty points with Wigan, Birmingham and Bolton. I reminded Keane that he'd promised the 'true Sunderland'.

'Yeah, well you have to be careful what you promise people but thank God … the players came up trumps today.'

Three days later, Kevin Keegan was appointed manager of Newcastle United.

TWENTY-THREE

Saturday 19 January and, for Sunderland, another trip to the capital. So far they had lost in London to Arsenal, West Ham and Chelsea. Now it was time for Tottenham again. On the opening day of the season Sunderland had famously beaten them 1-0, but now Spurs were managed by Juande Ramos, and were showing a marked upturn in fortune.

Before the match even started the news reached the press corps that Kieran Richardson was out again. He had pulled a hamstring in training and would be out for at least three weeks. On a miserably wet day in North London, Spurs heaped further misery on Sunderland when Aaron Lennon scored after just two minutes. Miraculously, Sunderland reached the break only one down but only a combination of profligate finishing and the heroics of Craig Gordon were keeping Sunderland in the game.

After the interval, Keane reverted from his 4–1–4–1 system to 4–4–2, and it was Spurs who found themselves beleaguered. Still, however, Sunderland just couldn't score, largely thanks to the brilliance of the Tottenham goalkeeper Radek Cerny. I like covering matches at White Hart Lane because, despite having to be a practising contortionist to squeeze into the Press seats, they are right behind the dugouts. You feel as though, with a good stretch, you could tap the manager on the back of the head. The only drawback is the fear that you are commentating loudly enough for the manager to actually hear what you're saying – and if the team is playing poorly this could be a severe blow to your working relationship. Thankfully, the only worry I had was when it was reported to me that, after another Sunderland near miss, my summariser, the former Sunderland centre-half Gary Bennett, had apparently used the 'f' word.

Cruelly the game was put beyond Sunderland in the ninety-third minute when Robbie Keane's speculative drive squirmed through Craig Gordon's hands. It was Keane's 100th goal for Spurs and it was fitting for it to come against his namesake.

The loss of Richardson was a blow to Keane but he was having none of it when I suggested, in mitigation, that he was cursed by injuries. 'No, I don't agree with that', he replied vehemently. 'I don't think it's about bad luck. I'm not going down that route. In football, all my life, you make your own luck. You defend like we did, particularly in the first half … Was it two minutes?'

I nodded.

'Away from home, defenders taking too much time on the ball and trying one or two tricks, that's not luck that.'

Life was getting tough. Sunderland were still firmly in the bottom three, the drop zone, and had now played twenty-three matches. But they were still level on points with Wigan and Birmingham. And now Birmingham were to be their next opponents at the Stadium of Light.

Further crucial signings were made. Phil Bardsley, a right-back from Manchester United arrived, as did the virtually unknown Swedish striker Rade Prica from Aalborg.

Sunderland badly needed a goalscorer, but Keane conceded that it was difficult to find one, and more significantly, difficult to pay the prices being asked, 'We have looked at certain strikers in the Premier League with proven goalscoring records, and we basically haven't been able to afford them.' Again, though, Keane underlined one of his big beliefs, 'First impressions are so important to me. They [Bardsley and Prica] have shown the desire and willingness that they want to come and play for Sunderland. I have to say, I have spoken to one or two players who asked too many questions really.' He added, 'I like players who just want to get on with it. Just keep quiet and get on with the job in hand, and these couple of players have shown me that in the first couple of days already.'

The first concern over Rade Prica was how to pronounce his name. After he had been called Preeka, Preacher and Prika, it was, after a consultation with the amiable Swede himself, established that it was pronounced 'Rada Pritza' and wasn't life on Wearside about to start well for the twenty-six year old.

The match with Birmingham City on Tuesday 29 January was the only home game of the season played midweek, and Birmingham turned out to be one of the poorest teams that came to visit. More was really expected of a team now managed by Alex McLeish. One of his first signings had been James McFadden from Everton, undoubtedly a classy player, but against Sunderland he foundered.

Daryl Murphy gave Sunderland a rare early lead when he tucked the ball away from six yards in the fifteenth minute, but, apart from a break from Cameron Jerome which led to a good save from Gordon, Birmingham rarely troubled the Sunderland defence.

Prica was introduced as a substitute at half-time and for fifteen minutes he looked hopelessly abandoned. When he did see the ball he invariably gave it away. In the sixty-third minute, however, Liam Ridgewell's header back to his goalkeeper was intercepted by Prica, who stabbed the ball past him to double Sunderland's lead. He almost added a dream second, minutes from time, but referee Mark Halsey deemed Prica had handled the ball before he poked it home. Unfortunately it proved something of a false dawn for the Swede and he barely featured for the rest of the season, but Keane was satisfied with his debut. 'I was tempted to start Prica', he told me in our post-match interview:

> ... but I think that would have been unfair. For any player to come to a club the hardest position is centre-forward, especially in this league. Even his first few touches he got clattered. But Bardo [Phil Bardsley, on his debut] has done very, very well. If you're going to play at full-back – and you're going to have a career – you've got to tackle, and Bardo likes to tackle.

Keane then made reference to there being too many full-backs who like to tiptoe around people and added:

> Bardo got a few tackles in. It lifted the crowd and then Prica came on and got one chance. Actually he had two chances, and took them ... probably unlucky not to have got the second one when we felt the referee was a little bit harsh to disallow it.

Such was the log jam at the bottom of the table that the win lifted Sunderland to fourteenth place. 'That's good', said Keane, 'I don't think the big four have to start worrying yet.' He added:

> People keep talking about what it's like to be in the bottom three and does it affect you psychologically, but let me tell you, if you win football matches, the table will look after itself. We've had a good result tonight but in one sense we have to move on very quickly … we've got a tough game on Saturday and we've picked up another few injuries tonight.

The tough game to which he referred was against Liverpool at Anfield, but it felt a whole lot better leaving the Stadium of Light that night, with Sunderland, at least for the moment, sitting mid-table.

There had been another departure. Keane had allowed Andy Cole to join Burnley on loan, feeling it unfair to keep him at Sunderland when he was getting so few opportunities, while still commuting from his home in the north-west of England.

The signing of Bardsley and Prica had taken Keane's spending since he arrived at the club in August 2006 to more than £40 million. Keane admitted, too, that he had been priced out of the market with some of his targets but that he would have no problem paying big wages to the kind of players who command them. 'If I was to sign [Christiano] Ronaldo tomorrow on £150,000 a week, I don't think our players would be upset', Keane said. Ironically, three months later Manchester United were reported to be offering Ronaldo just that figure to keep him at Old Trafford. At the time the highest paid player in the Premier League was John Terry of Chelsea on £130,000 a week.

Keane continued:

> It's none of their business. And the reason he would be getting that
> is because he's probably the best player in the world. I look at my
> own experiences. Somebody else's contract or wages is nobody else's
> business. If the lad next to me was getting twice as much as me I
> would say 'good luck' to him. Maybe he's got a better agent than me.
> Luckily I did have a good agent.

The bottom line at Sunderland, though, was that wages were a
stumbling block in signing new players. Keane agreed, 'As much
as we think sometimes we could try to afford the fee involved,
certainly the wages would be a big issue.'

Keane was happy with Prica and Bardsley. Bardsley, like last
season's loan signing Danny Simpson and the great Ryan Giggs,
was from Salford. Keane joked:

> Maybe I should go to Salford more often, because I think there
> they're tough lads and tough kids and what I call low maintenance.
> Just get on with the job. Not going on too much about conditions
> or who else I'm signing … as soon as I spoke to Prica (not that he's
> from Salford mind) and Bardsley they wanted to come to Sunderland
> and that'll do for me all day – straightforward deals.

TWENTY-FOUR

I always enjoy going to Anfield. It's a true football stadium and the atmosphere ahead of kick-off when the Kop sing 'You'll never walk alone' is electric. When footballers say they want to play in the Premier League they mean they want to play at Anfield or Old Trafford. When, or if, Liverpool leave Anfield for their new stadium, it just won't be the same. The history within the four stands at Anfield could never be replicated. If a stadium could be said to have a soul, Anfield has one. Highbury was the same. Sitting in the press box you are surrounded by Liverpool legends. The likes of Tommy Smith and John Aldridge sit shoulder to shoulder with you. The facilities have also improved of late. You used to have to squeeze into small wooden seats behind a tiny desk in a series of rows of desks beside the Directors' Box. Now the radio commentators have a spacious row all to themselves, behind the Directors, and right in front of the vocal Liverpool supporters. While the Press Box is home to a number of former Liverpool players, the Directors' Box is a veritable galaxy of stars. I've seen Chris De Burgh there a number of times. It is also generally a 'who's who' of football greats. That February night, amongst the scouts and the former Sunderland manager Denis Smith, was Sammy Lee. Later that season, Lee was to return to Anfield in the more formal role of assistant manager to Rafael Benitez.

Although the day had been warm and sunny, as kick-off approached on Saturday 2 February, it was darkening and the floodlights were ablaze. After the Birmingham win, Keane commented that Sunderland wouldn't be troubling the top four. Proof of this was soon to follow.

Sunderland lost 3-0.

Rafael Benitez gave Peter Crouch a rare start but it took him until the fifty-sixth minute to break down the Sunderland defence. A second goal was then added by the prolific Fernando Torres thirteen minutes later. After Sunderland had a solid penalty claim turned down by Rob Styles, who had punished Danny Higginbotham for a less obvious handball at Blackburn than this contact by Jamie Carragher, Nyron Nosworthy conceded a penalty at the other end in the eighty-ninth minute. Steven Gerrard converted with ease.

There was some irony in the penalty appeal being turned down by Rob Styles. Aside from the similar incident at Ewood Park, this was Styles's first match at Anfield since awarding Chelsea a controversial penalty there earlier in the season, handing them a point in a 1-1 draw. In a corner of Anfield's tiny press room, after Keane had spoken to the written press, he clearly hadn't forgotten the Higginbotham incident:

I'm sure that was the same referee today so I'm hoping to have a few words with him. There is a half hour, forty-five minute cooling off period. Not that I need to cool off, but I'd just like to ask him why one or two decisions we felt went against us, but I'm sure I'll get very little satisfaction.

A month or so later I asked him if in fact he had been to see Rob Styles that day. He had, and, much like Mick Jagger, he'd got no satisfaction.

More worrying for Sunderland and for Keane was the further injury to Kieran Richardson. The twenty-three year old had been out for barely three weeks when Keane named him in the starting line up at Anfield. Within five minutes, he was on his way back to the dressing room. The Sunderland captain Dean Whitehead told me Richardson had felt his hamstring go after thirty seconds and afterwards Keane admitted he'd rushed the midfielder back too soon.

The defeat saw Sunderland slip back two places to sixteenth, two points above third-from-bottom Birmingham City. Publicly, Keane remained unperturbed about Sunderland's flirtation with the relegation zone. 'I *am* quite relaxed about it, I have to say', he told the press before Sunderland's next game at home to Wigan Athletic, who'd beaten them 3-0 twice already this season. 'I'm okay with it. It might be different with two or three games to go but, at this moment in time, I am fairly focused.'

In fact, as it turned out, with five matches to go, he reacted angrily to complacency within the club, not just with the players, but his staff, in a public condemnation of a slackness he certainly would not have tolerated as the captain of Manchester United.

Now though, on Friday 8 February, the day before the Wigan match, he had nothing but good things to say, 'The group of players, I wouldn't swap them for anybody, [and] the staff and the supporters.'

At this time came the Premier League's proposal for the so-called 'thirty-ninth game'. In this proposal it was suggested that all the Premier League clubs would play an extra game, for league points, abroad. Widely condemned, it was expected Keane would condemn it too, but true to character, he thought the opposite. Keane also believed the club's fans would embrace the idea, perhaps for once in his life underestimating the feelings of supporters. But Keane's take was that, 'I know our fans and I know they would probably find a way of travelling in numbers, even if it is on the moon. Particularly if it is against Newcastle.'

Keane had also this season been taking his UEFA Pro Licence and, whilst enjoying it, concluded its value was limited, saying, 'they won't necessarily make or break you as a manager'. Yet again, Keane was to say in an interview published in *The Observer* on the weekend of the Wigan match, that he wasn't enjoying management. Indeed he said he was getting very little satisfaction from it at all. What, therefore, were his reasons for doing it?

I'm not sure. It's madness. You do it for the challenge. It's in you. It's a buzz. When I stopped playing I thought I could relax. But then I got this challenge from Sunderland. I enjoy the challenge, even if I get very little satisfaction from it. Maybe a five-minute taste when we win a game. That's why managers are old before they know it. What I love is being in a team game, being part of a team with coaching, medical and scouting staff.

Satisfaction was a theme that was to reappear at the end of the season. The photograph accompanying the *Observer* article showed Keane sporting a greying beard, more and more a feature of match days. As often as not, when I saw him first thing the day before a game, he'd be clean shaven. Twenty-four hours later he'd be sporting a beard that would take most of us a few days to grow. Intriguingly, for all the angst it obviously gives Keane, he told the press at his Wigan preview, 'I could have been on a beach. I could have stuck to my retirement. I could have taken it easy, but I wouldn't swap where I am now for anywhere else, I tell you. It's great.'

Against Wigan, Sunderland reversed what was becoming a trend by winning 2-0, the match most notable for Daryl Murphy's wonder strike for the second goal with fifteen minutes remaining. In fact, the goal won not just the game, but the *Match of the Day* 'Goal of the Month' for February. The club website, safc.com, run their own Goal of the Month competition, and the cameraman for the club Dan Makaveli and I had to laugh because Murphy's goal was only the second Sunderland had scored since 29 December. The club's competition was a foregone conclusion, so it was nice for Murphy to get recognition on a wider stage.

Wigan were actually unfortunate to lose, having hit the bar and the post and having a ball cleared off the line. Afterwards when I spoke to Keane, I pointed out that when the highlights were shown on *Match of the Day*, the game would look like a cracker. 'That's why *Match of the Day* is so good', he replied, 'They can squeeze a relatively poor ninety minutes into five or ten minutes and everyone will think it was a classic. But it wasn't a classic. It was ugly. It was tough.' He added, 'Sometimes you have to keep it tight and play ugly and we don't do that enough times. We see other teams do it near the bottom and getting results through it.'

Back up to fourteenth now, Sunderland were four points clear of Reading, who had been sucked into the relegation zone. With no away wins and no points away from home since September, a defeat at Portsmouth on Saturday 23 February would equal their club 'record' of ten successive away defeats.

An addition to the roster at the end of January had been the Charlton Athletic midfielder Andy Reid, another alumnus of Nottingham Forest and another Irishman. Recovering from injury, the twenty-five year old had made his debut as a substitute against Wigan and supplied the pinpoint long-range pass for Daryl Murphy to hit his twenty-five yard wonder strike. It was a brilliant pass. His twenty minutes against Wigan and his hard work in training earned him a first start at Fratton Park. One thing was clear about Andy Reid. He was overweight. Supporters can be cruel, especially those of the opposition and inevitably Reid found himself the butt of terrace humour. As far as Keane was concerned, 'the abuse should spur him on. I know it spurred me on.' Also, as far as Keane was concerned, the staff at the Academy of Light would make it their business to get Reid a little trimmer.

Reid was to prove an astute signing but, despite a good showing at Portsmouth for seventy minutes, the team as a whole let themselves down. When Kanu came on in the sixty-third minute they buckled. When the inevitable goal came it was from the sixth penalty Sunderland had conceded away from home, more than any other team in the league. Phil Bardsley tripped Niko Kranjcar in the sixty-ninth minute and Jermain Defoe converted the spot kick. Kranjcar had perhaps been slightly canny in winning the penalty, but, as Bardsley admitted later, any sort of contact in the penalty area is liable to be deemed a foul.

When Keane emerged from the dressing room into the narrow tunnel leading up to the pitch after his post-match television interview, he seemed a little tense. But it was only when he faced the written press in the Portsmouth Media Centre, as press rooms are increasingly called, that he let rip. He was furious and, with a direct reference to the introduction of Kanu to the match, said, 'some players can influence the game by just walking onto the pitch without actually touching the ball. I just hope that in future my boys leave their autograph books at home.'

With the next match to be played away from home, at rock-bottom Derby County, and with relegation clearly still an issue, I asked Keane if one win could change all their fortunes.

'We've been saying that since August', was the riposte, 'the season's nearly over now.'

TWENTY-FIVE

The match at Pride Park on Saturday 1 March marked Keane's eighteenth month as a manager. To celebrate, he would be returning to the ground where he had first named a Sunderland team. That time, his team had come from behind to win 2-1. Heading into the match this time it appeared there would be just two survivors from that starting line-up; Dean Whitehead and Liam Miller. However, six days before the game Miller was dramatically placed on the transfer list, the news breaking with a statement of just one short paragraph on the club website. Why? For repeatedly turning up late for training. When I saw Keane the day before the match I pointed out that the issue of Miller's transfer listing would be at the top of many supporters' agendas. 'It really shouldn't be at the top of people's agendas', was Keane's response. He continued:

We've got more important things to worry about, and that's getting a result on Saturday. I've made the position clear to Liam. One thing I've spoken to the players about on many occasions, and Liam in particular, is timekeeping. Nothing to do with talent but I've said if you want to be a top footballer you need a lot more than talent … and you certainly have to be on time for training. Liam has been late on a regular basis and I've got to be fair to everyone at the club. We will give the benefit of the doubt for once, twice, three times … four, maybe five times, maybe even six, maybe even seven. I am quite a nice guy. I don't go around looking for trouble. But if trouble is there you have to face it. But if you're driving to work, don't get into a car with Liam Miller because he gets involved in more car crashes than anybody I know.

This same week, it was also revealed that Keane had enlisted the help of the sports psychologist Bill Beswick. I had first met Bill when I covered Carlisle United, and Bill was a good friend of the then Carlisle United manager, Mick Wadsworth. On overnight stays for away games Carlisle would invariably stop at the Warrington College where Bill was Principal, to use the college football pitches for training. Bill Beswick's background was in basketball and when he retired from the college he pursued a career in sport psychology, and was often at Brunton Park. When Carlisle reached the final of the Autoglass Trophy against Birmingham City, at Wembley in 1995, Bill travelled with the team. I travelled with them also, and we all stayed at the Burnham Beeches Hotel, which Bill would get to know very well when he was enlisted by England and Steve McClaren. A day or so before the Wembley appearance Bill called the players and myself together in a downstairs conference room and gave us all a piece of wood about a foot square and several inches thick. He then convinced us all that we could smite the wood in two with just one swipe of the hand. Someone held the piece of wood so the flat face was horizontal. All but one of us succeeded.

Beswick also worked at Old Trafford when Keane was there and the latter has gone on record saying:

> I don't know if Bill played any part in me mellowing but I'd speak to him. It was all very casual. It wouldn't necessarily be about me mellowing. It would be all sorts. It was no major thing. If you wanted to go and see him you could and if you didn't, it was no big deal. I believe there is a place for that. I knew Bill well and at United he was very good. It was all very relaxed. Some people would see him once a year. Others would see him everyday. Some lads had no interest … Bill could tell someone he's the best player in the world and he'd probably believe it, but someone else wouldn't. I enjoyed speaking to Bill and I spoke to him when I first got the job here on a casual basis only. It wasn't all the psychological stuff.

Beswick's first job in football after his casual employment at Carlisle United was with Steve McClaren at Derby County. Keane said he'd 'spoken to players that knew him at Derby and appreciated his work there'. So, on 1 March, Sunderland and Keane were back at Derby. What had Keane learnt in the intervening eighteen months, I asked?

> I've learnt a lot, and you may say it seems a long time ago. It seems like yesterday to me and things happen very quickly in football … but we're all still learning. It's been a rollercoaster, shall we say, and I'm sure as long as I'm at the club it will be a rollercoaster. There

are going to be ups and downs and sometimes I think that's in the fabric of Sunderland ... and in a way I'm trying to change that. We're trying to build a solid team, where we can be very solid both home and away. At this moment in time we've not been able to do that, but we've an opportunity, like every away game, to stop the rot.

I then asked him how far down the road he thought he'd travelled. I added that with luck they would stay in the Premier League. He countered:

We've got nothing from luck ... You make your own luck. I think. When I became manager it was a three-year contract. First and foremost, part of the plan was to get back in the Premiership. We've managed to do that. The next step is to try and stay there and then to build on it. You could say we're probably on track for that, but things change in football. You're on about me making lots of changes. To be honest with you, I didn't expect to be making as many changes as I have done ... the danger in football is to plan too far ahead and things have happened at our club where I had to make changes last year in terms of personnel because of certain issues I wasn't happy with.

You asked me about Liam earlier. I have to look after the bigger picture and that's Sunderland football club. Some of my decisions, without doubt, won't please some of the supporters ... but as I've said before, I didn't come to Sunderland to be popular. I came here to be a success and try to get the team in the Premiership and stay there and be a stronger team ... and I think we're on track to do that.

Listen, there have been ups and downs. You look at this season. Our away form. Losing 7-1 at Everton. Losing to Luton. Losing at home to Wigan in the cup. Losing at home to [Manchester] United 4-0. I don't forget these things easily and they're more at my forefront than anything else. I keep saying I think the club deserves better than that and the supporters do … that's my job and that's why I enjoy that responsibility. In a sense I suppose I enjoy upsetting people. That's part of my nature I suppose.

As for the match itself, controversy was never far away and it reared its head after Michael Chopra scored in the thirteenth minute. A perfectly good goal as it turned out, but it was disallowed for offside. Mike Riley was the referee but the decision was made by one of his assistants. Keane spoke with Riley afterwards. He told the referee the goal was onside.

'Well Smartie told me at half-time that I got the call right', replied Riley.

'Excuse me, who is Smartie?' responded Keane.

Riley told him it was John Smart from Sky Television. He's instantly recognisable as he is often pictured close to the dugouts and has very distinctive white hair. Keane was less than impressed, 'If the referee is being influenced by Smarties what chance have you got? I haven't got a clue if they have it in for me or the club. Ask Smartie.'

Later in the week, following the game at Derby, Keane told me that 'five major decisions have gone against us. We keep talking about fairness but the decisions certainly haven't gone our way. You're looking at six points lost.' He added a *caveat* about Mike Riley, who had now officiated three Sunderland matches this season, Sunderland failing to score in all three, 'I spoke to Mike Riley after the Derby game, but you get little satisfaction because the game has gone. You end up feeling paranoid about things.'

A month later, the head of Referees, Keith Hackett, phoned Keane and apologised for the mistakes made against Sunderland. In the meantime Keane further added:

Since I've been in the job I've been to see three referees. That's not bad going really considering the decisions that have gone against us. I find it very hard to take some of the comments that come my way from referees and officials, and generally the attitude to our football club has left me very disappointed. The attitude seems to be 'It's only Sunderland'. All we're asking for is fairness in the game and this foot-ball club is not getting that at the moment.

TWENTY-SIX

Everton, of course, was where Keane had to endure one of the worst results of his career. Certainly, it was the worst result in his fledgling managerial career, and on 9 March, Everton were set to visit the Stadium of Light. It was scheduled as a Sunday afternoon kick-off as Everton were coming off the back of a UEFA Cup tie at Fiorentina, which they had lost 2-0, the previous Thursday night. That turned out to be an important result, not in terms of Everton's season as such, but in terms of how Everton were affected going into the match at Sunderland. The question would be whether Sunderland could capitalise on their opponents' mental and physical fatigue.

The game against Everton was the first of a trio of matches from which Sunderland were considered unlikely to take any points, the next two games being against Chelsea at home and

Aston Villa away. Sunderland were now only two points above third-from-bottom Bolton and the relegation zone. Thankfully, Bolton did not have a match at the weekend so there was no danger of Sunderland slipping behind them in the table. Bolton were in quite an unusual situation in that they were still in the UEFA Cup whilst fighting against relegation in the league. In their game against Sporting Lisbon, Gary Megson caused some controversy when he purposely fielded a weakened team to concentrate on the league. The arguments will rage on about whether he was right or wrong but Bolton finished the season strongly, while Glasgow Rangers, who lost in the UEFA Cup final, lost out in the domestic league title race to Celtic, and went from being strong contenders for a treble-winning season to coming away with only the Scottish Cup.

It seemed the ideal time to reflect on the game at Goodison Park four months earlier. I asked Keane if time had proved to be as great a healer as its reputation suggested. 'It's certainly *not* a great healer', he mused. 'I think – I've said it many times before – these are the games that you remember more than any other in your career.' His face was drawn and his gaze focused as he spoke. He would normally break into a smile or joke, but not today. As always, we had gathered in the narrow confines of the room in the Academy of Light, with the reporters from the *Sunderland Echo*, *Newcastle Evening Chronicle* and the club website, to preview the upcoming game. Keane would always arrive promptly, sailing through the media lounge almost unnoticed in his training kit, Louis Wanless by his side. Some days he'd be smiling and full of chat, but not every day. He said:

I don't know if it's a good or a bad thing that I remember the disappointments far more than the highs, and Everton is certainly one that will stick in the memory, no doubt till the day I die. That's the way it is and I'm sure it'll be the same for lots of the players, and no doubt the supporters. You've got to be hurt when you have days like this, but you have to move on. I learned a lot about myself that day, about the mistakes I made ... the most important thing is that you do learn from it. There's no point in having these bad experiences and going on to make the same mistakes over and over again. So we have to make sure, and I have to make sure, it doesn't happen again.

Did Keane make mistakes against Everton this time around? A lot of supporters thought so, as Everton won 1-0 with a scrambled goal from Andy Johnson just short of the hour. A clearly tired Everton team were not really challenged by Sunderland at all. Kenwyne Jones played on his own up front until late in the game. In the last few minutes Tim Howard tipped a free kick from substitute Andy Reid over the bar and Joleon Lescott cleared an attempt off the line, but it was just too little too late. Left-back Danny Collins, who was eventually named as the Supporters' Association Player of the Season, made the mistake that led to the Everton goal, and an Everton win.

While I also questioned the tactics in the game, with hindsight I can acknowledge Keane thought himself between a rock and a hard place against Everton. At 0-0 his system was working, but at 1-0 down he didn't want to repeat the mistake of Goodison Park, and go chasing the game only to lose more heavily as now goal difference was becoming an important criteria amongst the teams at the bottom of the table.

All the same, there was a general air of an opportunity lost and Keane himself perhaps felt the same. 'Mixed emotions really', he told me in our interview room just off the tunnel:

> I thought there weren't too many chances. We probably started pretty sluggish ... had a go the last ten or fifteen minutes. The 'keeper made a good save but again the goal has come from a bad mistake from ourselves. So, no one to blame but ourselves on that side of it.

I thought Keane sounded more down than usual after losing a game and said so. 'No', he answered:

> ... because, like last weekend, I think football's a cruel game. I'm down after every game. Sometimes the tone of your voice can be slightly different but I do believe the last weeks have been a bit unfair on the players. I've been honest. I've spoken to you after games where I've said 'no, I don't think we deserved anything today'. I'm not one for trying to make excuses, but I genuinely believe the group of players deserve better than what they've got last weekend and today ... The day you speak to me after a game and I'm not disappointed after a defeat it will be a sad day.

The same weekend Barnsley knocked Chelsea out of the FA Cup with a 1-0 win at Oakwell, but fortunately, it was Derby County who suffered the backlash, losing 6-1 at Stamford Bridge on the following Wednesday night.

The following Saturday, 15 March, the Stadium of Light was abounding with rumours before the Chelsea game kicked off that four players had been bombed from the squad for drinking ahead of the match. It completely took the edge off what turned out to be a very good game and spoilt the day for me; after the match, I would have to ask Keane if this was true. It was not something I was looking forward to.

To make matters worse, Sunderland lost 1-0 as a result of a John Terry header in the ninth minute. I had an uncomfortable feeling in the pit of my stomach when I set off down to the tunnel at the final whistle. In the days of Mick McCarthy, it was not unheard of to wait for up to an hour for an interview. Keane, however, seems to prefer getting his media duties out of the way quickly. I was grateful for this today, as waiting an hour with the question I was going to have to ask would have done my bowel no favours.

The first few questions about the match were fine. Then I said, 'Can I ask you about the players missing? Because inevitably there are rumours flying around the stadium about four players not involved today.'

I remember his brow furrowing and his pupils dilating.

'I don't know what you're talking about', he replied.

I ploughed on in a stumbling, fumbling way, naming the four players and adding, 'as I say, there are stories flying around. Are you able to, sort of, put that to bed?'

'What type of stories?'

You know that feeling when you wish you'd never started something? This was one of those occasions but I couldn't turn back now.

'The rumour is that they've been drinking and have been dropped from the squad for that reason?'

Keane's gaze remained intense.

'No. I've been in football a long, long time and that's the first time I've heard what you're saying to me there and it's the biggest load of nonsense I've ever heard ... Since I've been in football.'

'Thank God for that' I was thinking to myself, as it would save a lot of hassle and uncomfortable situations. But nonetheless I wasn't feeling at all comfortable at that moment in front of Keane, penned in by four or five other radio reporters and with Dan Makaveli filming it all for the club website over my shoulder. I did not get more comfortable as Keane continued:

> I think it's very harsh to be spreading rumours about four players who've been great ... I can only pick a squad of sixteen. That's what I've done and that was on the merit of what I've seen on the training pitch, and in the last week or two. One or two are still a little bit short on matches and I think these type of rumours are unfortunately a part of football. But absolute nonsense.

I felt compelled to add they weren't my rumours, but thought better of it, sensing it was a good time to bail out. As Keane exited the room to go and face the television cameras, however, I did holler, 'I had to ask, if nothing else to put them to bed ...'

He turned and smiled and said, 'Well, you've put them to bed' and he was gone out the door.

TWENTY-SEVEN

With the matches against Everton and Chelsea now behind them, Sunderland, were still two points above the drop zone. Aston Villa were in seventh and had lost the previous week to Portsmouth, exactly as had happened before their previous meeting when the two sides drew 1-1. This defeat by Portsmouth was only Villa's second defeat in their intervening fourteen league games since then.

As if the task wasn't hard enough, Kenwyne Jones was laid up the day before the game with flu, leaving Sunderland to start the game with Roy O'Donovan and Daryl Murphy in an all-Irish attack. O'Donovan, from Cork, is one of the nicest guys you could hope to meet. That impression was reinforced when I spoke to him at the Supporters' Association Player of the Year awards. He appeared to be really having a good time mingling with the supporters at the stadium that night and I told him so, adding the other players always moaned and groaned. He smiled and said he was enjoying it and the others 'say they're not, but they are really'.

As ever, O'Donovan worked his socks off, but just short of the hour he was replaced by Michael Chopra. Seven minutes from time Chopra ran onto a through ball and skilfully lifted it over the advancing Scott Carson. Martin O'Niell brought on Marlon Harewood to accompany John Carew up front for Villa, and Sunderland had to survive a few scares before full-time signalled their first away win of the season. Sunderland deserved the win, looking the more composed throughout, and the result saw them move to four points clear of Bolton, and three above Birmingham. Reading also now lay just one point above them.

Afterwards Keane acknowledged that it was 'a big three points, but the only time to really gauge it will be at the end of the season. I keep saying that'. He continued, standing at one side of the busy wide tunnel at Villa Park:

> Let's try and get to the end of the season and see how far we've come. It's a good relief for everybody and probably even more so for the supporters. I thought they were magnificent again today and it's great for them … they've spent an absolute fortune, I'm sure, travelling up and down the country, so it's nice for them to get their rewards.

The 3,000 Sunderland fans at Villa Park had been in such a good mood early on in the game that the tannoy announcer was driven to ask them to sit down, which inevitably had the reverse effect. Keane's own good spirits and relief were palpable when he spoke of Chopra's goal, 'We hung in there and got through a sticky patch and got one really good opportunity in the second half and, thank God, we took it.'

TWENTY-EIGHT

My pre-match interview the day before the home game with West Ham United on Friday 28 March was fairly run of the mill. Keane was in a good mood, sporting a new short haircut and a beard. It was rare that Keane didn't offer the press something to get their teeth into and today was no exception. The following day *The Sun* screamed 'Keano names and shames Fergie'. *The Star* kept to a more simple 'Hypocrites', while *The Times*, in keeping with the tone of the broadsheets, carried the headline 'Keane accuses Ferguson of setting poor example over referees issue'.

Very often the stories that emanated from throwaway remarks by Keane were made in the BBC Radio 5 Live interview with Juliette Ferrington, conducted on the dais in the small media theatre adjoining the media lounge. This time, Keane had been prompted to attack managers for paying lip service to the idea of respecting match officials while actively undermining them.

'There are a lot of hypocrites in football', were his reported remarks. 'A manager was talking last week about respecting referees. The same manager has been sent off this season for foul and abusive language.' This was a clear reference to Sir Alex Ferguson's dismissal at Bolton in November, when Mark Clattenburg sent him to the stands. 'If managers don't respect officials how can you expect players to?'

Keane implied further criticism of Ferguson following the Manchester United manager's outburst after the FA Cup defeat by Portsmouth at Old Trafford. 'I don't think any manager should have any power above anybody else', he said, adding 'United had twenty chances to score during that game and didn't take any'. He went on to say that Ferguson's outrage had surprised him and that 'Manchester United always taught me to be a gracious loser, but they weren't that day.'

Inevitably Keane's railing against Andy D'Urso at Middlesbrough in 2000 was highlighted in many papers, but not the fact that Keane is now a staunch ally of the Football Association's 'Respect' campaign. As to the criticism of hypocrisy, he responded, quite simply, that 'I was a player then and I'm a manager now.'

Keane now rigidly applies these standards to his players and staff, 'If I thought for a minute that Ricky [Sbragia] and Tony [Loughlan] were abusing officials I'd stop it in a second ... I don't want anyone abusing officials at this club. I spoke to my staff about respecting referees in my very first week in the job.'

The same morning Keane confirmed his interest in signing Jonny Evans on a permanent basis. It would have been interesting to have heard the reaction to that at Old Trafford in the light of Keane's veiled attack. Of course, Ferguson knows Keane only too well and is no stranger to the outspokenness of his former captain. In fact, it was that trait that led to Keane's departure from Manchester United.

Only a few days later, Keane met Tom Humphries of *The Irish Times* at the annual Irish Guide Dogs for the Blind convention in Dublin. He told him:

… the day I left United, in hindsight, I should have stopped playing really. I lost the love of the game that Friday morning. I thought football is cruel, life is cruel. It takes two to tango also. I am fully responsible for my own actions but some things are wrong. I left on a Friday and they told me certain things before I left that day. I was told the following week I couldn't sign for another club. I had been led to believe I could. There were certain things I was told at certain meetings that were basic lies.

They had a statement prepared and they were thanking me for eleven and a half years of service. I had to remind the manager and David Gill [Manchester United Chief Executive] that I had been there twelve and a half years. I think that might have been part of the plan. Then financial stuff was mentioned. I was thinking, 'my God, I am happy to leave'. I won't go down that road. A week later they announced £70 or £80 million profit after telling me I hadn't played for six weeks and so they weren't prepared to do this and that. I told David Gill I had broken my foot playing for Manchester United against Liverpool. Pretty sad.

And so, on to West Ham United. So far this season, the Hammers had not lost a single game in which they had taken the lead.

Sunderland, for their part, hadn't won any game in which they had gone behind. At 1-1 in stoppage time, the match seemed to be heading for a predictable draw when Andy Reid kept his head and drove a low shot past Rob Green from twelve yards. Sunderland won 2-1. It was also the sixth time this season that Sunderland had scored in stoppage time.

'Oh it was a big, big goal for us', said Keane in the aftermath. 'A big goal for the season. I think in the history of the club maybe.' The win lifted Sunderland seven points clear of Bolton who were now still third-from-bottom. He continued:

> I thought we started really badly ... gave a shocking goal away and managed to get an equaliser very quickly and changed things a little bit in terms of the players at half-time ... you always felt when you saw the five minutes going up for injury time, just give us one more chance, and that's what we got. That's why we brought Reidy to the club. He's capable of producing.

Straight after the game, the players flew to Spain for a few days of warm weather training. Such practices are becoming more widespread even in the Championship, where Phil Brown (South Shields born and manager of Hull City) put his team's superb run to the play-off final and subsequent promotion down to a break in Dubai in January. Keane, as might be expected, was quick to dispel any suggestion that it was a holiday.

TWENTY-NINE

Having broken their away duck at Aston Villa, Sunderland's next away game, on Saturday 5 April, was at relegation-haunted Fulham. Fulham were bright and lively and driven by Jimmy Bullard in midfield, but it was Sunderland who hit the net first when Danny Collins – a 66-1 long shot to score the first goal – headed past Kasey Keller. Mark Halsey, however, ruled it out. Collins was not to be deterred, though. Over recent weeks, he had been getting closer and closer to scoring, and on the stroke of half-time, he finally did so.

It was a major blow to Fulham whose seven-year stay in the Premier League appeared to be coming to an end. The points were effectively sealed for Sunderland when substitute Chopra came on to lob Keller in the fifty-third minute. In the seventy-third minute, a Fulham fight-back was launched when

David Healy scored with a memorable twenty-five-yard drive, but it was all in vain as two minutes later Kenwyne Jones wrapped it up. This left Fulham six points from safety with only five matches remaining. Crucially, as it turned out, two of those five games were against relegation rivals, Reading and Birmingham City. Sunderland were now ten points above the relegation zone.

'I'd rather be ten points clear than ten points behind,' Keane laughed, 'but if I've said it once I've said it a million times, we've some tough games coming up. But we're heading in the right direction.'

It hadn't been a particularly good display against Fulham, but, as Keane added, 'the big difference today – we scored goals at the right time. As much as I was disappointed with the performance today, they had that desire to carry on and get goals and win the game.'

The staff at Fulham had resigned themselves to relegation, as had manager Roy Hodgson. Over the next few weeks, though, it was all to come together for Fulham, just at the same time as it all began to unravel for Sunderland.

Anyone, myself included, who dared suggest that Sunderland were safe now received short shrift from Keane. If the manager needed any proof to justify his warning that Sunderland were far from safe, it came against Sven-Göran Eriksson's team. Manchester City had only won three times away from home, but in the seventy-eighth minute, they took the lead with a penalty from Elano. This penalty was the eighth of the season awarded against Keane's team. Three minutes later Dean Whitehead pulled Sunderland level with his only goal of the season, but, three minutes from full-time, Darius Vassell took all the points with a scrappy goal.

'I've been saying it all week,' Keane said to me afterwards with a glint of menace, 'and hopefully the players and the staff will be picking up what I've been trying to say. We've got a lot of hard work ahead and we want to make sure we're in the Premiership next year.' His analysis was succinct, 'I think we took our eye off the ball today. Very sloppy.'

With four matches left, Sunderland were now only five points above the bottom three. Birmingham now occupied the last relegation berth and Bolton had climbed a point clear. Sunderland were three points behind Newcastle United and their goal difference was worse by just one. Only once had Sunderland been above Newcastle all season, for just twenty-four happy hours, following victory over West Ham on 29 March. Sunderland had elevated themselves a point above their arch rivals that day, only for Newcastle to confound everyone the next afternoon, including possibly even Kevin Keegan, when they won 4-1 at Tottenham.

On Sunday 20 April Sunderland could once again leapfrog Newcastle with victory at St James' Park. The omens were not good though, with rumours all week that Jonny Evans was injured. This was confirmed to be the case a couple of hours before the scheduled kick-off at half past one, but the news was worse. A knee problem meant Phil Bardsley's appearance against Manchester City was his last of the season. Danny Higginbotham replaced Evans, and Paul McShane, who hadn't played since January, replaced Bardsley at right-back. A more positive omen was that Keane had played at Newcastle twelve times, eleven times with Manchester United and once with Nottingham Forest. He'd only lost twice – the two times he was sent off.

Sunderland's record at Newcastle was better than at home. Fans still fondly recall the night of 25 August 1999. That day, during a rainstorm of biblical proportions, Sunderland beat Newcastle 2-1, with goals from Kevin Phillips and Niall Quinn coming after Kieron Dyer had given Newcastle the lead. Critically Ruud Gullit, the Newcastle manager, had dropped Alan Shearer and Duncan Ferguson. In a gamble that backfired disastrously, he played Sunderland-born rookie Paul Robinson in attack. Gullit resigned three days later.

There was another significant moment in the derby of August '99, with Sunderland leading 2-1. Kevin Ball (currently assistant Academy manager), playing in the Sunderland midfield, had put in a crashing tackle on Duncan Ferguson. The ball ricocheted some forty yards and was sailing over goalkeeper Thomas Sorensen's head for a Newcastle equaliser. Miraculously it hit the bar. Kevin Ball retells the tale every year there's a derby and it gets funnier every time. The punchline always has me in stitches, as Kevin, in a mock Danish accent mimicking Sorensen, says 'I had it covered'. It was an incredible night and anyone there will never forget it. I was pleased that it was memorable, as I was so drenched by the rain my notes disintegrated.

The derby is a fixture from which the fans expect passion, spirit and endeavour. As Keane had said ahead of the match in November, 'we need leaders, warriors'. To all eyes it seemed Keane was lining up with a 4–4–1–1, or 4–5–1 formation and to everyone's surprise Chopra was on the bench. Liam Miller was instead recalled from exile, his first match since February. Within three minutes, Sunderland went a goal down when Michael Owen got ahead of Paul McShane and guided his header beyond Craig Gordon. And Sunderland just didn't respond. A minute before the break Danny Higginbotham haplessly got caught by the ball striking him on the arm, as it had at Blackburn, and Owen coolly converted the penalty.

Sunderland played better in the second half but never really with conviction. Craig Gordon saved excellently at close range from Obafemi Martins in the sixty-seventh minute and a minute later Steve Harper did likewise from Kenwyne Jones. Chopra didn't come on until the eightieth minute.

Sunderland fans left St James' Park bewildered and angry. To be honest, in the light of the defeat I wasn't brave enough to ask Keane about his tactics. Throughout the week, however, they became the main topic on the radio phone-ins and on supporter message boards. I resolved to ask him later that week, when we met to preview the next match, at home to Middlesbrough. In the meantime, straight after the match, Keane spoke to me in the corridor that runs behind the stage of the Newcastle United media room.

'We played a lot better second half but we were two down and sometimes it's slightly easier to play in that sense.' In contrast to the hubbub around us, he was quiet as he spoke:

No, we gave two bad goals away at two bad times in the game ... and I've had this conversation before with you. You want to start the game as well as you can and to be a goal down after three or four minutes in a derby match is always going to be hard. Then to make it even worse, to concede just on half-time ... So we made it very hard for ourselves.

Five days later, first thing on the Friday morning, I steeled myself to ask about the formation at St James' Park.

'There's a lot of talk', I nervously proffered, 'of perhaps the wrong tactics ... 4–4–2 more advantageous?"

'Well, what system do you think we played?' Keane immediately replied with an intense glare, challenging me to back up my claim.

'... one up front with possibly [Andy] Reid just behind that ...'

'Yeah ...'

Several seconds of horrible silence followed, with him fixing his gaze rigidly on me. Finally he went on:

> Yeah, that was the system we played and people are entitled to their own opinions. When you don't win a game of football people are going to analyse it and criticise. And I've absolutely no problem with that. But we felt that was the right way, the way the team had trained that week ... I think the goals we gave away were no reflection.

If Keane had initially been annoyed at my question, which he was, he was now calmer and his usual relaxed self:

> It has absolutely nothing to do one way with the system we played ... Absolutely none whatsoever. When you win it's great. When you lose you're going to be criticised. I have absolutely no problem with that. It's part of the job, but we felt it was the right tactics and it was the right team and we gave two bad goals away. At that level you never win a game of football.

To borrow a phrase from *Hamlet*, I immediately thought Keane 'doth protest too much'.

THIRTY

A win at home over Middlesbrough on Saturday 26 April, as long as some other games being played went their way, and Sunderland would secure their Premier League status. Both Middlesbrough and Sunderland were on thirty-six points, five points above Birmingham City and Birmingham were up against the might of Liverpool.

Sunderland did not start well. Tuncay scored for Middlesbrough after only four minutes. The Black Cats responded in style, however, Danny Higginbotham equalising a minute later from Danny Collins's cross. The stage was set for a rousing match. Sunderland took the lead for the first time in the forty-fifth minute, when Chopra, restored to the starting line up, scored from close range. The striker nearly doubled the lead in the sixty-seventh minute, but was denied by a brilliant save from Brad Jones. Meanwhile Birmingham were 2-0 up at Liverpool.

Fulham, two down at Manchester City and looking lost, were also fighting back and pulled themselves level at 2–2.

Then, in the seventy-third minute, Afonso Alves equalised for Middlesbrough.

And then Liverpool had pulled a goal back at Birmingham.

Now in a dramatic three-way finale, Fulham scored a last-ditch winner at Manchester City; Liverpool equalised at Birmingham, and in the ninety-second minute at Sunderland, for the ninth time in the season, Sunderland scored at the death. Substitute Daryl Murphy met Grant Leadbitter's corner to head powerfully over the line. The referee was Steve Bennett and all eyes immediately looked to him now. It was several long seconds before he gave the signal, and the goal was given. With the goals coming late in the other matches, the players had been left a little in the dark in the dressing room as to whether or not Sunderland were safe. Poor Mark Boddy, who compiles the statistics, saw his job and his good looks hanging by a thread as he got in a muddle over the results.

But Sunderland were safe.

Keane left the dressing room beaming. He thanked the assorted staff who had gathered about. By the time he reached me in the former 'Entertainers' room at the end of the tunnel, his face had been restored to a familiar post-match rigidity.

I picked up on a point in the game when it was 2–2 and both managers could have settled for a draw, which Gareth Southgate certainly did, but Keane surely decided to try and win it. 'Most definitely', he concurred:

Trust me, that was going through our heads. I spoke to the staff a little bit and we were saying 2–2, and a home game, you know. We've got Bolton next week and Arsenal coming up and that. I think that, as the home team, we were probably criticised by a lot of people, particularly through the media and one or two of our supporters, for negative attitudes last week, which I certainly wouldn't agree with – yourself being one of them…

I'm sure I went bright red as Keane continued, 'but I think when you're the home team you have to go for it'.

With Premier League status assured there was suddenly a little time for reflection. Keane continued:

We've had some bad luck, a lot a lot of bad luck this season. I know you've got to make your own luck but hopefully we won't be in this position next season. But, like I've said before, we need to strengthen. We need to improve because today, with three games to go, we're down to the bare bones. You just have to look at some of the other squads in the Premiership and you admire them because sometimes it comes down to the last two or three weeks – who's got the strongest squad. We've managed to get over the finishing line and that's all credit to all my players and the staff. The staff have been brilliant.

Sunderland were now safe from relegation but there were still two games to play. Keane added:

Well I can try and relax … I will definitely enjoy it tonight and tomorrow. I think the most relieved people on the planet will be my wife and kids because unfortunately they're the ones who suffer. We look forward to it, but the beauty of football is that there's another challenge next week. If anyone thinks we're going to go down there

[Bolton] with the attitude of 'I've taken my foot off the gas' then that would be disrespectful to our supporters and we certainly won't do that.

Keane was asked if he felt satisfied by the season.

'Satisfied actually would be a very good way of putting it', he replied, 'I'm not a great one for enjoying things too long … we've got to move on and get ready for next season'. Keane laughed:

I might have tomorrow off … No, no … it's amazing because we've had talks this week and I spoke with Niall [Quinn], but everything's been on hold until we got over that finishing line. But now talks can take place over the next week or two and full steam ahead for this football club to get bigger and stronger.

The talks would be coloured by events that were to unfold the following weekend at the Reebok Stadium.

THIRTY-ONE

Saturday 3 May was sunny and warm. Summer appeared to be finally on the way. Sunderland's penultimate match of the season had been moved to 5.15p.m. by Setanta Sports, clearly in the belief there would be plenty riding on the outcome for both clubs. As it transpired, there was certainly plenty riding on the outcome for some of Sunderland's players, but it was only Bolton Wanderers for whom the result was ultimately important. The match that Setanta probably should have screened was the one at Craven Cottage where Fulham beat their relegation rivals Birmingham City 2-0 to, incredibly, lift themselves out of the bottom three for the first time since December.

Before the previous game, Keane had warned that Sunderland were not safe. Now he warned that if any players showed a lack of commitment at the Reebok Stadium they could find their bags packed. Permanently.

In front of a packed stadium and the live television audience, Sunderland were abject. One seasoned Sunderland observer told me it was one of the worst performances he had ever witnessed. At the end of the season Niall Quinn told me that it was for him, as a performance, worse than the 7-1 drubbing at Everton and the defeat at Newcastle. These were strong words indeed, when you consider that after the Newcastle match, Quinn had to witness United Chairman Chris Mort leading a conga through the boardroom.

Sunderland lost to Bolton 2-0. The closest they came to a goal was an 'air kick' from two yards by Kenwyne Jones, almost comical in its execution. Keane was furious. When he spoke to me in the spacious tunnel outside the Sunderland dressing room his eyes sparkled with anger. By the time he'd reached the media room on the third floor this anger was flooding out. He accused his players of 'switching off'.

'Does that mean people think survival is something to celebrate?' Keane spat. 'If they do I don't really want them at the club. There will be changes. Trust me. I've no problem getting rid of players with four years on their contracts. We'll just give them a few bob to go', he snarled. 'This has confirmed how short we are. It needs to be sorted.'

A few weeks later Sunderland released their retained list and, apart from the four players whose departure had already been announced (Stephen Wright, Andy Cole, Stan Varga and Ian Harte), everyone in the established first team squad was listed apart from Dwight Yorke. The reason for his omission was that Yorke and Keane planned to spend some time discussing the Trinidad and Tobago international's future. Yorke had offers from

Australia to consider, while Keane was hoping to persuade Yorke to stay to pursue a coaching role. Yorke came out of international retirement at the beginning of June to play twenty minutes of a friendly against England. In the same match, Kenwyne Jones damaged ligaments in a collision with David James. It was particularly harsh on Jones who hadn't wanted to play in the meaningless match, and it left Sunderland worrying whether one of their key players would be fit for the start of the following season. The fact that the retained list named everybody, and that included the players such as Greg Halford, Graham Kavanagh and Russell Anderson, and the Spaniard Arnau, who had all spent long spells out on loan, meant nothing. There was no question that a number of them would not be at Sunderland for the start of the next season. As contracted players, however, Sunderland would just be looking to get transfer money for them. After the last game of the season, Keane met with Niall Quinn and Chief Executive Peter Walker, and made clear the players he was happy to see leave.

Sunderland had lost twenty-two matches this season, including the Cup matches with Wigan and Luton. And Arsenal was still to come. After the Bolton game Keane remarked that he was 'lucky to be in a job'. Even in anger he doesn't lose his capacity for humour, which is just one reason why he's such a hit with the press. He delivered again at the Reebok, adding how his children probably hated him as a parent but not as much as the players would if he was their parent!

Bolton, meanwhile, were technically safe. It would take an extraordinary set of results to sink them the last weekend of the season. These would kick-off the next weekend, simultaneously now, in deference to Sky Television, on Sunday afternoon.

The following Thursday I was to meet and interview Keane twice in one day. The first meeting, at a 8.45a.m, was to preview the final match at home to Arsenal. I wondered if the comments made by Keane in the heat of the moment in the aftermath of the defeat at Bolton still held true. But firstly I thought I should ask whether he had spoken to the players. His reply was cheerful:

Not really. I think it's important now that we try and focus on the game on Sunday and have discussions with certain people next week. I'll have to take most of my action, I think, after the final game of the season. What I said after the game last week hasn't really left me. As manager of the football club I have to be honest. You're saying 'critical' of the players. I don't think I … was I critical of them? Maybe I suppose I was but … I've defended them long enough this season. But last week's performance, as manager of the football club, I have to say if it's not good enough. You can't keep trying to kid people all the time, and last weekend wasn't good enough. That's what I said after the game and I think people shouldn't have a problem with that really.

Keane reflected for a moment on this, but quickly returned his thoughts to the match at Newcastle United:

We want to lift the standards of the football club and we dropped our standards last weekend – we certainly did, and we can't get away from that. We've got to be big enough and honest enough to accept that … the manager and the coaching staff get criticised (probably after the Newcastle game in terms of the system we played) but it goes to show we played two up front last weekend and it didn't change the result, did it? So that's why I say people have to be careful when they start talking about the systems. It does come down to how players adapt to it.

He added:

Since I've become a manager, and I appreciate I've only been a manager for two minutes, I really haven't regretted too many of my comments straight after a game. I genuinely think my gut reaction is not far off the mark ... there probably have been occasions, certainly after this game, where I've kept my head. I've said we need to move on quickly and sometimes, as part of the game as a manager, you have to try and kid people. But I wasn't really in the mood to do that last week and, as I said, as manager of the football club I think I've every right to do that. You're saying it's three or four days after the game, but that feeling hasn't left me. I'm still pretty angry about it to be honest with you.

I asked Keane if the game against Bolton had refocused decisions he needed to make about the squad? He replied in a shot:

One hundred per cent. I think, I hate saying it, but it was probably a good thing what happened last weekend. I think particularly while I'm going to be manager of this football club. Because possibly if we got a good result against Arsenal next week we might have gone to the end of the season saying 'maybe we're not far away' but last week showed me that ... I wanted to see a Sunderland that was more relaxed; players who wanted to have the ball, who were happy to play in tight situations, who were happy to keep it. Basically since I got the job we've always been nearly in a 'must-win' situation. Last week, we went into the game and I was hoping to see another side to Sunderland, one that would be more relaxed and, I suppose, more entertaining. And we didn't see that. We just saw that one or two of the results we had were covering the cracks that we already knew about, so it's just confirmed … but it's about action now.

I think the supporters, a lot of people, have had false dawns at the club and I've been saying it, that we all have to be patient. But I suppose if I was a supporter out there, they're probably saying 'we've been patient quite a long time'. You can't keep saying that, so it's up to me to make the changes. Last weekend, on reflection, believe it or not, will probably be a good thing for the long term future of the club, especially while I'm manager here … it confirms we have to make changes.

It was not the preface to the Arsenal game everyone had envisaged. Keane made five changes. Hungarian international Marton Fulop played his only Sunderland game of the season, and possibly his last. Ross Wallace played for the first time since 2 January, having recovered from a broken leg, and Dwight Yorke returned to the starting line-up.

A sell-out crowd of 47,802 watched Arsenal win 1-0 with a piece of magic from nineteen-year-old Theo Walcott, in an entertaining but low-key end-of-season match. Elsewhere there were twists and turns but, as Keane had long predicted, Manchester United won the title. Fulham won their last match of the season at Portsmouth by a single goal, but, despite hefty wins for Birmingham City (4-1 at home to Blackburn Rovers) and for Reading (4-0 at Derby County), both were relegated.

Keane saw no reason to celebrate a season which ended with Sunderland finishing in fifteenth place. With thirty-nine points, they were three behind Middlesbrough who thrashed Manchester City 8-1 in Sven-Göran Eriksson's swansong. Sunderland also finished four points behind Newcastle United. Before that final match, Keane told me:

> I honestly think there's nothing to be celebrated. It was like last year when we went up and we were getting invites to go here, and open-top busses and I was like, 'that's nonsense' … getting promotion shouldn't be seen as a celebration of a football club like Sunderland, and staying in the Premiership shouldn't be seen as a celebration. I think I naturally must be a very miserable person. There's no getting away from it.

Nevertheless, there was a smile on Keane's face when he joined the players to walk round the pitch following their final game. He reflected:

> I think I have enjoyed the victories. I've enjoyed the challenge of keeping the club in the Premiership, enjoyed the end of the game, walking around and seeing the players with their kids and seeing the reception they received … there's been some good moments. I will probably reflect better over the next week or two when I'm away from the club and with my own family. So overall, satisfied … try and learn from the mistakes that I've made and make sure the club is in a much stronger position next year.

THIRTY-TWO

My second meeting with Keane on that Thursday before the match with Arsenal was in the afternoon, in the 'Parents' Lounge' at the Academy of Light. We were due to meet at 3p.m. to record an end-of-season review for the Sunderland website. I waited with cameraman Dave Cave. And we waited. And waited. And paced in and out to the balcony overlooking the training pitches basking in mid-May sunshine. Had he forgotten? An hour later he arrived straight from his office clasping a bottle of water, and couldn't be more apologetic. He'd been caught in a meeting.

Mic'ed up and on a high stool with the training ground as a backdrop through the lounge's glass doors, I asked him how tough it had been in the previous close season to attract the players he wanted. His reply was now, after eighteen months, a familiar retort:

I think it's tough for every manager. I think every manager would like to draw up a list of players he'd like to bring to the club and just sit back and hope it falls into place. But it was very difficult, and understandably so because of the fact that we'd just got promoted. Also a lot of players would be reluctant to come to a club that's just been promoted, especially a club like ourselves that has been promoted many times and relegated – so it was very, very tough. Having said that, going into the season I was fairly happy with the group of players we had. I think from day one we knew it was going to be a long hard season. I just knew it was going to be very tough. There's such a big gap between the Championship and the Premiership.

It had always been my feeling that the win over Tottenham Hotspur on the opening day of the season was one of the most significant results, and I asked Keane, echoing his thoughts on the game at the time, how important it had been to hit the ground running:

I think it was vital that we got a victory under our belt very quickly because previously the club had struggled. You look at the points total they had the previous season – was it fifteen? – and we just knew we hoped to at least do better than that, and we felt we would because we did bring in a lot of players. We just hoped that they would gel pretty quickly ... and it certainly helped that Chopra scored in the first game of the season, and we got a late equaliser the following Wednesday.

And what about the late goals? Nine in all, in the final five minutes or added time. Was that luck?

We're delighted we scored so many late goals, but we don't want to be getting ourselves in that position again next season because it is very hard. All credit goes to the players for that. Their drive and their will to get something out of a game, particularly at home … we always felt in the last ten or fifteen minutes that we looked like we'd get a few goals. But we needed that away from home as well, so all credit to the players for that … they show that everyday in training. Their attitude is generally very, very good.

Conversely, though, Sunderland didn't score many early goals and had been notoriously slow starters, I remarked. Keane agreed:

No. We never really got to the bottom of it … trust me, we've looked at it, we've discussed it. We've tried different stuff. You look at the warm-ups, at their preparation the day before the game. We've analysed on every side of it but sometimes it comes down to the players and, sometimes, just concentration levels … We conceded very quickly at Tottenham, at Newcastle, at home to Middlesbrough, probably a number of other games I can't really think of off the top of my head. So that was a big problem for us. As much as we're delighted with the late goals we got, we have certainly got to cut that out in our game.

Importantly though, I said, in all the games Sunderland took the lead, they held it.

Well, of course that's been one of the positives, and there have been lots of positives. I know that after one or two of the defeats we tended to focus a lot on the negatives, but there have been so many positives. To get eleven victories, we always knew it was going to be hard. One of the disappointing aspects of the season has been the lack of ability to grind out results, particularly away from home, when a lot of times we were in a good position perhaps to get a draw, which we never took. So that's all part of the learning curve for myself and the staff. I remember we went down to West Ham and got it back to 1-1 and we were thinking we must go on to win the game. But we get hit with the sucker punch and lose 3-1 when maybe a draw would have been fine. I look forward to the season coming up where you think you'd probably take a draw away from home in nearly every game. It would have had a big influence on our season, trust me, because we've lost far too many games. But, as you said, there've been lots of positives and hopefully we'll all learn from this season.

Sunderland finished the season in fifteenth place, but, I pointed out, if you added the points for the disallowed goals, and the goals allowed, such as that at Reading, Sunderland would have finished the season a few places higher. Keane laughed:

I'd forgotten all about them. Yeah, but it's all ifs-and-buts. Over the course of a season you're going to get decisions like that which go against you. Maybe one or two, I think, we were slightly unlucky to have. Maybe four or five really big decisions go against us, but imagine if we hadn't scored the late winners? It's all ifs-and-buts. If we are to finish fifteenth I truly believe we're probably the fifteenth best team in the League. I've said before that over the course of thirty-eight games the table doesn't lie. We can look back and say we were a bit unlucky there, disappointed with decisions gone against us, look at our injuries, but I don't think the table lies, and we'll finish where we deserve to be. I wouldn't say we're happy to be fifteenth, but we're satisfied. But we certainly won't be settling for that next season.

I asked Keane if he'd learnt more from the defeats than the wins. He agreed straight away:

> Most certainly. I think you always do in life. You learn a lot more from your setbacks than the highs. We have to make sure we don't make the same mistakes next season, because if we do then clearly we haven't learned, so that's one of the bits of information we've learnt … and, trust me, there has been a lot to learn.

Inevitably, with the numbers of players Keane had brought to the club over eighteen months, there were going to be successes and failures, but I asked him if he would agree that he had, on the whole, got the key signings, such as Kenwyne Jones, Craig Gordon, Phil Bardsley and Jonny Evans, right and at the crucial times. The Corkman's verdict?

> Most certainly. We were fortunate … We just got Kenwyne coming into the season, because we knew we lacked someone with a physical presence. We had Stern John but we knew Stern was going to be heading the other way to Southampton. So … players come in at the right time. Just like last year, I think particularly in January, we brought in Jonny [Evans], Simmo [Danny Simpson], Carlos Edwards, and of course the same again this January. Reidy [Andy Reid], and Jonny coming back … and Bardo [Phil Bardsley] … and Rade [Prica] coming in and scoring an important goal for us. You have to remember a lot of the positives these players have brought to the club … really this summer, I don't want to be signing as many players as last year. I think it's very hard to bring that amount of players into a club and try and gel them together, but what we do want to do is bring in a lot of quality players with a lot of expe-

rience. You're probably looking at six or seven players, whereas last year I must have brought in, I would have thought, about fourteen or fifteen. Having said that, I think we needed them because we were short, particularly going into pre-season when as early as a week or two into the season, we picked up a few injuries – and major injuries to Kieran [Richardson], Deano [Whitehead], Carlos [Edwards]. So we were stuck, and lucky we brought that amount of players in.

Craig Gordon had arrived with a £9 million price tag on his head and he didn't really get the benefit of a settled back-four until January. I asked Keane if he felt that that was significant:

Of course … in a sense you're chasing your tail all the time. We're making changes. We're expecting a young goalkeeper who we believe, with a bit more experience, will become a top, top goal-keeper – one of the best in the world without a shadow of a doubt – but it was hard for him when we were turning into a team that was struggling and sometimes lacking a bit of confidence, particularly away from home. But he's come through it and he will be so much better for it next season. As will the likes of Kenwyne, because, we have to remember, it was his first year in the Premiership as well, and even young Jonny coming in – they're all plusses. We have to remember the plusses.

Keane had described managing in the Championship as the easy part, as managing in the Premier League often centred on a specific 'major' moment in a match which could turn out to be critical.

They're vital, yeah, very much so. I'm not trying to be blasé about the Championship – I wouldn't say it was easy to manage, but I knew once we got that momentum, with the size of the club and the supporters behind us and one or two players, I knew the team wasn't as bad as the first four or five defeats suggested. So I meant that in a nice way, but also knew that when we got promoted, that this is where the real work starts. Because we're in the Premiership. You look at the top four teams, two of them in the Champions League final. At this moment in time it's the toughest league in the world. We knew it was going to be hard and just like this year we've managed to stay in the Premiership, we know next year is going to be harder. So we've got to learn from the mistakes we made. There was a big plus in getting promoted so quickly, but it was all part of my challenge really, as I said when I signed a three-year deal here. I thought first and foremost 'let's get promotion'. We happened to do that pretty quickly, thank God. Second season, make sure we stay in the Premiership. But next year we want more. I'm sure the supporters are thinking exactly the same.

One of Keane's fundamental challenges was to try to change the mindset at Sunderland football club after years of false dawns and failures. It's been a challenge to alter the attitudes of the players, but I remarked to Keane that he'd also worked to change the attitudes of the press and media, and the supporters. I recalled after the home game with West Ham United how we, the media, had made the assumption Sunderland were safe, but he rejected the notion angrily and has always striven to reinforce a winning psychology.

Of course ... that's been the biggest challenge since I've come to the club ... changing the mindset of everybody I work with ...

throughout the last few years, particularly at Sunderland, any little bit of success – when I say success I mean promotion – has been followed by doom and gloom and relegation. Even when it was confirmed we were in the Premiership a couple of weeks ago … I never thought that was for one minute a time to celebrate. I really don't feel it's anything to celebrate. And that goes for everybody at the club … people who work at the club, like yourselves through the media, you're trying to change everybody to say, 'listen, that's what we expect at the football club, it's nothing to be getting too excited about'. Yeah, the lads should be fairly satisfied but to say we're happy and we can celebrate against Arsenal and sit back and relax, far from it, you can't relax in this game. You've got to go full steam ahead and that is trying to speak to Niall [Quinn] and to Peter [Walker] and get everyone to try to think as positively as me.

In the light of that I asked Keane if he felt he was making headway:

Yes, we are making progress but it hasn't not been easy, trust me, because a lot of people have been set in their ways. It's just what they've been used to. It's been the same with some of the players at the club. Remember Deano, Grant, Nyron, Danny Collins, the only experience they've had in the Premiership has been losing … losing most weeks … so we're trying to change that. Hopefully they'll be the wiser for it next season. Like I've said from pre-season, we've earned the right, so let's go, let's not step back and get bogged down by the fact we're in the Premiership. Let's go and make our mark. We have done that in certain games. We've missed out on other opportunities but, fortunately for us as a football club, we've got another opportunity to do it again next year and make sure we are progressing. We have to aim higher in the league, and that's maybe mid-table, I don't know. We definitely have got to do better in the Cups. We're not satisfied with that side of it since I've come to the club. We're Sunderland and we should be looking forward to this challenge. We shouldn't be afraid of it. We're not far away, but we're far enough away.

As he lowered himself off his stool Keane offered his hand for only the third time since I'd met him back in August 2006. He apologised again for being late and I said, 'don't worry … at least you turned up.' He laughed and said there was no fear of him not doing that, 'unlike maybe a few years ago'. He turned to go and spied a bookshelf of novels left for the parents and Academy players. He stooped to lift one off the shelf and joked they were far too advanced for footballers! Then, seconds later, he headed back down the corridor to his office.

EPILOGUE

Back in August 2007, I was asked on the BBC Radio Newcastle breakfast show where Sunderland would finish in the Premier League. I said thirteenth. I believed then, and I remained solid in my belief through the season, that Sunderland would stay up. In the end they finished fifteenth, but had the goal against Aston Villa at the Stadium of Light not been ruled out and the goal at Reading in December not been ruled in, then Sunderland would have finished at least thirteenth if not twelfth. Perhaps above Newcastle United.

It was certainly a rollercoaster ride and, for me, there were two pivotal periods in the season. The first was the first game of the season when Sunderland beat Tottenham with Chopra's last-gasp goal. Keane had insisted Sunderland had to hit the ground running and to have lost on the opening day would have been a major setback. It gave everyone belief and that was critical. The second moment was in January, and the transfer window signings of Jonny Evans, Phil Bardsley and Andy Reid. Those players cemented the team. The defenders steadied the back four and gave Craig Gordon the confidence he had so lacked in the first four months. Reid unlocked the midfield and finally the forwards found a little more freedom. They weren't prolific but they scored some vital goals. Reid himself contributed one of the best moments of the season with his winner ninety-five minutes and twenty-four seconds into the game against West Ham at the Stadium of Light.

Clearly, though, there were plenty of occasions when the team didn't deliver. Bolton Wanderers at the Reebok Stadium was a match that, for me, established Kieran Richardson as a player who may not make the grade if Sunderland steps up a level, as Keane demands. Despite his injuries, he didn't convince me he has the attitude to be a winner. I always recall that he played in the Manchester United team at Old Trafford that failed to beat Conference Exeter City in the FA Cup, and to me that's very telling.

Anthony Stokes again failed to turn training-ground brilliance into anything like Premier League consistency. Liam Miller is almost a good player but of course has fallen foul of Keane's rigid discipline. He may yet establish himself but the chances are he'll move on. Carlos Edwards has just not had the chance to re-establish himself and ultimately I think Dean Whitehead and Grant Leadbitter had poor seasons. On the plus side, Kenwyne Jones proved to be an excellent acquisition and once Gordon gained his confidence he proved himself a brilliant 'keeper. I've mentioned Bardsley, Evans and Reid, but Danny Collins has knuckled down since he won his place back and deservedly won the Supporters' Association Player of the Season award.

Keane has always insisted that the core of a solid team is in place and I'd have to agree with that, on the condition that everyone remains fit and available. However, there has been an inconsistency which I don't necessarily think was due to tactics or teams but to attitude, and on too many occasions the players didn't show the spirit for which they've become renowned. That may be due, in part, to what Keane referred to at the end of the season; the players who've become used to playing in losing teams. He has had to sign players of a better quality, players who have Premier League experience at successful clubs, whether they were mid-table or in the Champions League, and of an age where they can give Sunderland a solid three to five years service.

There have been some incredible moments this season, particularly all of the late, late goals. In all there were nine scored in the last five minutes or added time plus another three in the last ten minutes. A remarkable record.

The lowest moments were, of course, the 7-1 defeat at Everton, the poor display at Bolton and the limp effort at St James' Park. That Newcastle game was very hard to take. I think Keane really understood what that fixture meant after the fall-out from that match, which included a difference of opinion with me over the tactics and formation he played that day.

Soon after the end of the season Keane holidayed for a week in Dubai before flying on to New Zealand to complete his UEFA Pro Licence badge. Ironically, he spent a week with the New Zealand All Blacks in the lead up to their Test match with Ireland. Graham Henry, the All Blacks coach, joked, 'We have probably got similar views [on refs]' but more seriously added:

… he has been great, great to talk to, very bubbly. Everyone knows him and respects him for what he has done in sport and it's great that he chose, along with Ricki Herbert [New Zealand and Wellington Phoenix coach, also completing his Pro Licence], to be here with the All Blacks as part of their requirements for their final coaching certificate in football.

Throughout last season, especially in the context of conversations I had with colleagues from around the country who deal with Premier League and Championship managers, Keane remained brilliant to deal with and I'm really looking forward to our conversations again in 2008/09. Keane will then be fully qualified to manage in the Premier League for many years to come and I'm sure his reputation, and his team, will only grow and grow.

SAFC 2007/2008

Statistics

Wins: 11.
Draws: 6.
Defeats: 21.

Yellow cards: 60.
Red cards: 5.

Consecutive wins: 3.
Consecutive away defeats: 10 (equalling the club record).

Wins after being behind: 2.

Penalties
For: 2 (one converted).
Against: 9 (all converted).

Number of players used: 31.

Most appearances: Danny Collins, 35.

Fewest: Russell Anderson, 1 and Stern John, 1 (substitutes).

Leading goalscorers: Kenwyne Jones, 7. Michael Chopra, 6.

Goals by Substitutes: 9.

Goals scored in the last five minutes: 9.

Goals conceded in the last five minutes: 7.

Points earned from last minute goals: 11.

Points lost from last minute goals: 2.

Biggest win: Sunderland 3-1 Bolton Wanderers, Fulham 1-3 Sunderland.

Heaviest defeat: Everton 7-1 Sunderland.

Clean sheets: 7.

Transfers

Roy Keane ended his first Premier League season as a manager with the promise that he wouldn't be rushed into signing new faces in the close season. He was true to his word. He flew to Dubai for a week with his family at the end of May and it was late July before the first of ten new players arrived, though two of the ten, Nick Colgan and David Meyler, were clearly fringe players. Of course there was plenty of speculation as to who would come in, but Keane was adamant he wanted quality not quantity.

Sunderland travelled to Portugal for early pre-season training. Unfortunately a sending off for Michael Chopra led to an early-season suspension for the striker, whose troubled private life came to prominence at the end of August when he checked into the 'Sporting Chance' Clinic with what the football club described as 'personal issues'.

Once back from Portugal, the promised players began to filter through from the unexpected direction of North and East London. A trio arrived from Spurs; Pascal Chimbonda, Teemu Tainio and then Steed Malbranque. They were followed from Bolton by El Hadji Diouf. Keane promised more arrivals; the football world took notice and the supporters were thrilled when Djibril Cisse arrived on loan from Marseille and David Healy was signed from Fulham.

By now the season had begun and it was clear that a striker was a priority, especially with the absence of Kenwyne Jones who was out for at least two months following his injury in a friendly for Trinidad and Tobago against England in the Caribbean at the season's end. Keane's spending wasn't over. Just before deadline day, after much speculation, Anton Ferdinand signed from West Ham and he was followed on deadline day by former Sunderland left-back George McCartney, who'd left only two years previously and had been a fans' favourite.

There was traffic out of the club as well. Early departures were Ross Wallace to Preston and Greg Halford to Sheffield United on season loans. They were followed by loans of Russell Anderson to Burnley, Arnau for another season at Falkirk, and the likeable Irishman Roy O'Donovan to Dundee United. Latterly Paul McShane moved to newly promoted Hull City, a move announced on the day Hull were given a reality check by Wigan Athletic who beat them at home 5-0. The only player who left Sunderland on a permanent basis was Danny Higginbotham, who returned to Stoke only a season after leaving and almost a year to the day that had he made his Sunderland debut at Manchester United.

Keane had talked of kicking on from the last season, and the quality he brought to the club in the summer was evident in the first two matches of the season – at home to Liverpool and away at Tottenham, where Sunderland had not won in the top flight for thirty-nine years. The three former Spurs players made their debuts against Liverpool, as did El Hadji Diouf, following a successful pre-season that had included a tour of Ireland and matches against Nottingham Forest and Ajax. As successful as the pre-season matches were, Roy Keane was to lament after the Liverpool game that perhaps it hadn't been testing enough. The reason was plain to see, as Sunderland tired against Rafael Benitez's below-par team and lost to a late Fernando Torres strike. However, the performances of the four debutants illustrated the fact that Sunderland had stepped up a gear from the previous season and the match boded well for the future.

Further evidence was provided at White Hart Lane, where, very soon into his Sunderland career, Pascal Chimbonda learnt the hard way that timekeeping is one of Keane's particular foibles. The French defender was two minutes late for the team 'stroll' at the hotel on the morning of the match and was dropped. His place was taken by Phil Bardsley and the soon-to-depart Danny Higginbotham, who was wearing the shirt for the last time at left back (though he was on the bench for the Carling Cup tie at Nottingham Forest and against Manchester City).

Djibril Cisse made his first Sunderland appearance at White Hart Lane as a second-half substitute and, as he had done for Liverpool against Spurs, scored on his debut. It proved to be the winner; a reborn Kieran Richardson, who'd had a good pre-season following a season dogged by his back problems, had given Sunderland the lead with a wonder strike. Sunderland won 2-1. The opening two matches provided a glimpse of a tougher, grittier, more rounded Sunderland.

That work still needed to be done was proved by the matches at Nottingham Forest and Manchester City. Sunderland had to dig deep to beat Nottingham Forest, doing so in extra-time with a goal from debutant David Healy. They folded against Manchester City in the second half, losing 3-0 the day before it was announced that City had been taken over by a Dubai-based billionaire who instantly smashed the British transfer record by signing the Brazilian Robinho from under the nose of Chelsea for £32 million from Real Madrid. That same day, Manchester United finally prised Dimitar Berbatov from Spurs, beating Manchester City who had also made an outlandish bid for the Bulgarian.

The beginning of September heralded another chapter in the history of the Premier League and another in the history of Sunderland, as Keane told me he was glad to see the back of his players for a few days and left to take stock of the remaining thirty-five matches of his second season as a manager in the Premier League.

> If you think you are beaten, you are.
> If you think you dare not, you don't.
> If you like to win, but think you can't,
> it is almost certain you won't.
>
> Life battles don't always go to the stronger or faster man,
> but sooner or later the man who wins
> is the man who thinks he can!